P9-DGJ-788

the graduate institute for world affairs
NUMBER 2

EXPLOSIVE FORCES

IN

LATIN AMERICA

A Publication of the
Mershon Center for Education in National Security

EXPLOSIVE FORCES

IN

LATIN AMERICA

Edited by

John J. TePaske and Sydney Nettleton Fisher

Ohio State University Press

Publications of the Graduate Institute for World Affairs

1. The Military in the Middle East: *Problems in Society and Government,*
edited by Sydney Nettleton Fisher

2. Explosive Forces in Latin America

PREFACE

THE EIGHT PAPERS included in this volume were first presented November 1-3, 1962, at the second annual three-day conference of the Graduate Institute for World Affairs of the Ohio State University. "Explosive Forces in Latin America" was the general theme of the conference. There were four public sessions with two papers delivered at each meeting. Discussion leaders commented on individual papers, and each session concluded with comments and questions from the floor.

The authors have revised their papers in the light of the discussions at the conference, adding new material as it seemed relevant to emphasizing points made in their original presentations. Wherever possible, they have included references to more recent events which have modified or confirmed previous conclusions. The role of informal conversations outside of scheduled meetings of the conference also should not be overlooked in evaluating the views and ideas expressed.

Editing has been kept at a minimum and has largely
served to bring some uniformity to the volume, although the
individual styles of the authors have been preserved. In some
cases the authors have expanded their original papers to
explain points more clearly and to include further references that give new or broader dimensions to their theses.

The authors and editors acknowledge their indebtedness
to the public and private comments of all who participated
in or attended the conference. They appreciate, particularly,
the contributions of those who chaired the sessions and of
those who initiated the discussions: Dean Richard Armitage,
Ohio State University; Dr. Frank B. Berry, Department of
Defense; Dr. Herbert E. Evans, Peoples Broadcasting Cor-
poration; Professor Charles P. Loomis, Michigan State Uni-
versity; Dr. Otis A. Maxfield, First Community Church,
Columbus, Ohio; Professor John L. Phelan, University of
Wisconsin; Professor Frederick B. Pike, University of Notre
Dame; Professor Robert E. Quirk, Indiana University;
Professor William S. Stokes, Claremont Men's College;
Professor Erik Thorbecke, Iowa State University; Professor
Kempton Webb, Columbia University; Professor A. Curtis
Wilgus, University of Florida; and Dr. Bryce Wood, Social
Research Council.

JOHN J. TePASKE
SYDNEY NETTLETON FISHER

CONTENTS

EXPLOSIVE FORCES
IN
LATIN AMERICA

SOVIET POLICY
FOR
CASTRO'S CUBA

DAVID D. BURKS

SOVIET interests and strategy in Latin America have undergone basic revisions since 1959, as the result of the Cuban revolution led by Fidel Castro. Furthermore, Soviet successes and failures in exploiting the Cuban revolution have changed, in some very important ways, the nature of the problem facing the United States in Cuba and elsewhere in the Americas. The events of the last three years have required a re-evaluation of Soviet policy in the Western Hemisphere and the importance of the Cuban revolution as an instrument of that policy. Today, as a result of the missile crisis of October-November, 1962, both the United States and the Soviet Union have reached a crossroads in their positions on the Cuban question.

The Cuban policy of the Soviet Union passed through three distinct stages in the years 1959-1962. During the first stage, which lasted through most of 1959, the Russians did little to aid and support Castro overtly, although they welcomed the leftward shift of his policies. In the second period, beginning early in 1960, the Soviets exploited Castro's willingness to turn to the communist bloc for economic aid, military equipment, and diplomatic support. This phase ended with the disaster of the Bay of Pigs. The third stage was an aftermath of the abortive Cuban invasion. The Russians came to believe that the United States would tolerate Castro, given the proper Soviet diplomacy. They concluded that they could build infinitely stronger ties with Castro without spurring the United States to drastic retaliation. The missile crisis, however, has initiated still a fourth stage in Soviet-Cuban policy, but its full outline has not yet become apparent either from the welter of post-crisis Soviet propaganda or from new Soviet actions.

I

During the first year of the Castro regime, the Russians viewed the Cuban scene cautiously. Soviet leaders were undoubtedly intrigued by Castro's early drift toward neutralism in the Cold War, but initially they were hesitant to believe that he would be useful. Moreover, the Castro government could not at first be called communist, although the *Partido Socialista Popular* (PSP, the Communist Party of Cuba) rapidly gained in its efforts to indoctrinate those around Castro and to infiltrate the regime. Surely Soviet intelligence must have been aware of the growing conflict between the Communists and anti-Communists within the Cuban government and the PSP's concern over Fidel's predilection for implementing radical programs very rapidly, regardless of

4

the economic cost. On the other hand, the Soviets feared justifiably that Castro might turn on the PSP, using his immense personal power over the Cuban people to crush the Cuban communist movement.

During most of 1959, therefore, the Russians confined their efforts to advising the Popular Socialist Party through a number of transmission belts. Probably the most important Soviet effort of this kind was sending a number of Russian, Eastern European, and Latin American advisers to Cuba. The Russian trade-union delegation, for example, which "observed" the congress of the Cuban Confederation of Labor in November, 1959, also advised the PSP.

The official communist line in 1959 identified Castroism as a national liberation movement. An article in the January, 1959, issue of the *World Marxist Review,* the major international communist ideological journal, portrayed events in Cuba as part of a hemisphere-wide pattern of unrest, which included a wave of strikes in 1957 and 1958, the overthrow of Rojas Pinilla in Colombia in 1957, and the ousting of Pérez Jiménez in Venezuela in 1958. According to this article written by Pedro Reyes, remaining Latin American dictatorships would inevitably be replaced by bourgeois or national democratic governments, typical of national liberation movements. The basic controlling forces in Latin America were the latifundists, the *comprador bourgeoisie* (bankers, foreign traders, executives of foreign and mixed companies, and their lackeys), and the United States government. Eventually these groups would be overthrown in order to attain that "economic and political independence . . . which is . . . the principal national task of the Latin American countries at the present stage." The tactic advocated by Reyes to

5

gain these ends was the popular front, used so effectively in the 1930's and now named the "united front." The united front would set as its goals economic and diplomatic relations with the communist bloc, "democratization of the state system," democratic agrarian reform, and a higher standard of living. Such a front would be constructed on the broadest possible popular base with a program couched in phraseology designed to quiet fears of a communist take-over.

The industrial proletariat, "the decisive force in industry and agriculture" in Latin America, would dominate the united front. Guided by the communist parties, the proletariat would seek to ally with any major component of society that was able and willing to battle the influence of the United States. Unfortunately, stated the article, the disunited peasantry was presently asleep and could be aroused only by agrarian reform. The chief ally of the Communist-led workers, therefore, would have to be the national bourgeoisie, the nationalistic element of the professions and business. In the long run, however, the national bourgeoisie would prove an unreliable ally because of its ambivalence on many questions. The inability of the bourgeoisie to follow a fixed policy, Reyes affirmed, stemmed from the fact that although its interests were often in conflict with those of American capitalists, it was dependent in many ways upon foreign economic interests.[1] As presented in the *Review,* this communist program in Latin America did not demand rigidity in the face of local conditions confronting each national communist party; on the contrary, the plan stressed flexible adjustment to national variations and idiosyncrasies.

Signs of change in Latin America, heralded by *Pravda* as the arrival of spring, occurred simultaneously with the general relaxation of East-West tensions.[2] Krushchev's visit to the United States late in 1959 and the Soviet exhibitions in New York and Mexico City softened Latin American resistance to the blandishments of the communist bloc. Russian propagandists effectively harped on the theme that emergence of neutralist and reformist governments in Latin America lay just over the horizon, because the balance of power in the world was now tipping in favor of the Soviet Union. Soviet propaganda highlighted reports that Latin Americans wished to co-operate with the Afro-Asians at the United Nations, a move which would reduce the "mechanical majority" of the United States, although, in fact, only Cuba voted with the neutrals at the UN General Assembly in the fall of 1959.[3] In October, 1959, *Kommunist,* the official ideological journal of the Communist Party of the Soviet Union, placed Cuba in a list of some eight neutral countries along with the United Arab Republic and Iraq.[4] The United States, insisted the Russian propagandists, would resist these neutralist tendencies with all the pressure she could apply. Continued military domination of Latin America was absolutely essential for the United States and a foretaste of threats which neutrals of other continents could expect.[5] Soviet propagandists also made partially successful appeals to Afro-Asian neutralists to identify themselves with Cuba and thus accept the proposition that defeat of the Cuban revolution would endanger them also.[6] According to the Russian line, the United States first sought to gain control of the revolution by means of economic aid. When this approach failed, the United States turned to economic blockade and military threats, justifying them by allegations of international communist influence in the Cuban government. Deriding the fable of the communist

7

danger in Cuba, *New Times,* a Russian communist journal written largely for foreign consumption, stated in August, 1959, that not a single Communist held an official position in Cuba. Through the rest of the year, the Russians maintained this position.[7]

Although the value of Castroism was readily apparent, the Kremlin was probably not as optimistic about springtime in Latin America as its official propaganda indicated. Castro's Cuba, as she moved to neutralism in 1959, represented a major break in the solidarity of the Americas in the East-West struggle. As a revolutionary, Castro persistently sought in 1959 to export his very radical revolution in a manner likely to stimulate similar upheavals in other countries in the hemisphere. Not only would a Pandora's box be opened for the United States, but Latin American Communists would find rich opportunities to better their positions.

Initially the Castro revolution was placed in the broader context already described. In 1959, the *World Marxist Review* and other communist publications did not look upon the revolution as the chief focus of communist efforts in the Americas. Following the traditional communist policy throughout Latin America, the Communists had aimed at domination of labor in Cuba, a country where the peasant had played a minor role in national life in recent years. This was in sharp contrast to Castro's view of his revolutionary base as peasant and petty bourgeois. The Communists also sought to participate actively in political life by operating as a legal party and by the formation of political alliances, not by going to the mountains to fight.

8

II

The next stage in Cuban-Russian relations began dramatically in February, 1960, when the Russians seized the initiative from the United States. Boldly grasping the opportunities offered by Castro's growing estrangement from the United States and the expansion of communist influence in his government, Khrushchev sent his famous "traveling salesman," First Deputy Premier Anastas Mikoyan, to Havana to strengthen Russian-Cuban ties. In Cuba, Mikoyan was warmly received.[8] He negotiated trade and aid agreements with the Cubans during his visit;[9] and in May, 1960, diplomatic relations were formally re-established between the two nations.[10] For the Russians, Cuba now became a Latin American pilot project, a model to prove the value of diplomatic and economic relations with the communist bloc. The example, it was hoped, would attract the many Latin American nations dependent upon a depressed world market for the sale of large amounts of agricultural products and other commodities.[11]

Another major Soviet objective at this stage was to use Cuba as a center for hemispheric communist activities. Russia continued to welcome Castro's efforts to turn the Andes into another Sierra Maestra. Significantly, the first Russian ambassador assigned to Cuba had, in the 1940's, been in charge of the Soviet spy ring in Canada.[12] A host of communist operations, from front groups to Spanish language publications, was moved to Cuba. Two currents of agitation thus flowed from Havana—one communist, the other Fidelista. Though they sometimes merged, they remained, nevertheless, separate and still distinguishable.[13]

Soviet objectives in Cuba had expanded but were still checked by Soviet fear of United States reaction. The Russians remembered the fate of the Arbenz government in Guatemala, which, when it fell in 1954, had reached a point of heavy communist infiltration.[14] While it lasted, the Arbenz regime had been a highly useful tool for various propaganda and subversive purposes. The Soviets supplied "technical assistance" by sending skilled party leaders from other countries, including a number from Cuba, who gave the somewhat backward Guatemalan Communists guidance on strategy and tactics and helped to resolve factional disputes. Direct aid by the Soviet bloc never went beyond one shipment of Czech arms to Arbenz. This one move, however, was enough to arouse the United States into action that helped to bring down the Arbenz regime.

The fall of Arbenz led some communist strategists to propound a policy of geographical determinism. This theory held that in countries as close to the United States as Cuba and Guatemala, anti-United States governments could not survive. After 1954, geographical determinism became especially popular with a number of extreme nationalists, leftists, and Communists in Latin America.[15] Whether the Soviets ever accepted the theory is difficult to determine, but they seem to have believed in 1960 that the United States would stand for only so much in Cuba; yet they were willing to test the limits of American patience. This approach was Lenin's policy of applying and fitting Marxism to differing objective realities. An excellent example of Soviet cautious exploitations of Castroism occurred in June, 1960, when Khrushchev accepted a request to visit Cuba.[16] When he failed to secure similar invitations from other Latin American nations, he

10

postponed his trip.[17] A visit solely to Havana would have destroyed the myth perpetuated by Soviet propaganda that Russia had widespread support in Latin America. It would also have identified Cuba as the only close ally of Russia in the hemisphere.

The doctrine of "peaceful coexistence" as propounded in the 1950's tended to make the Soviets more adept in their Cuban policy. "Peaceful coexistence" is essentially an aggressive doctrine; while ruling out major war, it attempts to upset the status quo to Soviet advantage. Thus, in "colonial" areas like Latin America, coexistence seeks to encourage the appearance of national liberation regimes. Such regimes are valuable to the Russians because they are willing to become neutral by breaking what, in the Soviet view, are long standing ties of dependence upon the United States or other "imperialist powers."[18]

In the second stage of Russian policy, memories of Guatemala and the obvious overwhelming American power in the Caribbean seemed to outweigh the doctrine of coexistence. The Russians were apparently as convinced as many Cubans that the United States would eventually resort to military action to destroy Castro. Throughout 1960 and the first months of 1961, Russian propaganda stressed this point in increasingly strident and vituperative tones.[19] Their aid to Cuba also reflected this view. In early summer, when the Cuban government seized foreign oil refineries, the Russians responded quickly to meet Cuban crude petroleum needs. They justified their actions as the usual Soviet policy of supporting countries seeking "independence" in foreign affairs. Russian propaganda branded the ending of the American quota for Cuban sugar as an American reprisal

11

for Cuban petroleum policy. Conflict over sugar brought Cuba to the United Nations with charges of United States aggression, but the Russians abstained on permitting the complaint to be removed from the Security Council to the Organization of American States. The Soviet Union, however, slowly moved toward a mildly protective stance for her Caribbean protégé. In a Security Council debate on June 19, the Soviet representative stated that Russia might assist Cuba militarily if asked, but added that this was not a threat to use rockets.[20]

Within a few days, however, Khrushchev enlarged the Russian commitment by saying, "Figuratively speaking, if need be, Soviet artillerymen can support the Cuban people with their rocket fire, should the aggressive forces in the Pentagon dare to start intervention against Cuba." This statement contained some broad loopholes which were enlarged by the addition of the adjective, "symbolic," in a *Pravda* story. It was later revealed that Khrushchev had, in fact, narrowed the interpretation when he clarified his remark for Cuban newsmen. By "symbolic," he stated, he meant that he hoped the Soviet Union would never have to use the rockets to defend Cuba.[21] In the United States, President Eisenhower responded that the United States would never tolerate an international communist regime in the Western Hemisphere. For his part Khrushchev contended that the Monroe Doctrine had died a natural death; but, he asserted, Russia did not desire and did not need military bases in Cuba, and Castro's was not a communist revolution.[22]

Apparently the Cubans jubilantly misinterpreted the Soviet premier's remarks and believed that Russia would agree to a bilateral military pact or even admit Cuba to the Warsaw Pact.[23] Succeeding months proved Moscow was not willing to be so adventuresome; the arguments against an alliance were overwhelming. For the Russians, apparently, nothing seemed more suicidal than to place in the hands of an "unstable" Castro the trigger of a gun pointed at the United States.[24] In the past, the Soviets had undertaken such solemn military obligations only with communist countries they controlled. Probably the conclusive factor negating an alliance was Soviet belief that the United States would eventually move to destroy the Castro government. As a substitute for a dangerous military pact, Russia began heavy shipments of arms to Cuba in the summer of 1960.[25]

The Russians were still eager to have Cuba serve as an example of the progress a Latin American country could make once it had liberated itself from United States domination. They did not, of course, reject Cuba as an alternative prototype for revolution but preferred to play down the communist role in creating the revolution because of the unpopularity of communism with much of the middle class in Latin America. The Soviet hope that the nationalistic sector of the bourgeoisie would push for an anti–United States policy continued to be strong. In December, 1960, the Russian government and the Cuban economic mission, led by Ernesto Guevara, visiting Moscow issued a joint communiqué that highlighted the Cuban revolution as an important example of a national liberation movement not only for Latin America but also for Asia and Africa. Yet during this visit, the Russians allowed Guevara to move toward a different position. In reference to the declaration of eighty-one communist parties setting forth communist objectives and

13

methods, he stated that although "we took no part in this declaration we support it with all our hearts."[26] The propagandists in Moscow also vigorously protested the charge of international communist infiltration in Cuba and in the Americas levied by the United States at the San José conference in August, 1960.[27] The *New Times,* in March, 1961, characterized the Cuban revolution as a nativist movement with roots in Latin American reality, rather than one inspired by foreign Communists.[28]

III

The failure of the April invasion at Playa Girón (Bay of Pigs) inaugurated the third stage in Russian policy for Cuba and the hemisphere. This fiasco enabled Russia to escape the obligation to deliver on promises of "symbolic rockets—or to back down. But at that, the Russian premier was cautious. On the second day of the invasion, he sent President Kennedy a note charging the United States with responsibility, demanding that the invasion stop, and promising to give the Cubans "all necessary assistance." He did not repeat his rocket threat.[29] Castro's proclamation on May 1, 1961, that Cuba was a socialist state was acknowledged by the Soviet press without editorial comment.[30]

Soon, however, Khrushchev began to pursue a bolder course. In conversation with foreign newsmen after Playa Girón, the Soviet premier openly expressed his inability to understand why President Kennedy had not either refrained from invading Cuba or carried it through to completion. At the Vienna meeting with the American president in June, Khrushchev reportedly found him indecisive. One can only

14

conclude that the Soviet premier had begun to believe that Cuba could be closely tied to the Soviet bloc and yet coexist with the United States, given the proper Soviet diplomacy.[31] Thus Soviet moves which had begun as a series of probing actions to test the courage and resourcefulness of the United States now initiated a crucial new phase in Soviet diplomacy with implications for the Cold War everywhere.

The new policy was outlined in the June issue of the *World Marxist Review* in an article entitled "Crushing Defeat for Exporters of Counter Revolution."[32] The article hailed the Cuban revolution as the first completely victorious anti-imperialist movement in the hemisphere. The Cubans, it stated, had destroyed for all time the geographical fatalism which, prior to April, had inhibited the growth of national liberation movements in Latin America. The *Review* went on to say that President Kennedy, advised by Barry Goldwater, Nelson Rockefeller, Richard Nixon, and former President Eisenhower, had concealed the American role in the invasion because open participation would have brought "a powerful rebuff from the socialist countries." The socialist countries, for their part, would have helped Cuba anyway if aid had been needed, but the Cubans had successfully defended themselves because their revolution was native, national, and not imported. This propaganda preserved the fiction that communist military might had been ready and available to help the valiant Cubans.

The Russians evidently believed, as their diplomats stated privately, that it was time for the United States to reconcile herself to the existence of a communist state in the hemisphere and to "coexist" with it in normal relations, particularly economic. Although no one was certain how rapidly

15

Cuba's economy was deteriorating, any restoration of trade with the United States would have been invaluable for Castro and the Soviets.[33] According to widespread rumor, Guevara secretly requested United States economic aid when he attended the Punta del Este economic conference in August, 1961.

Moscow interpreted Washington's policy as one of irresolution. Russian leaders did not accept at face value the American insistence after April, 1961, that self-restraint in the Cuban case was not weakness. For its part, the Kennedy administration maintained that the issue of communism in Cuba was not negotiable and continued the policy of seeking legal and economic sanctions against Cuba through the Organization of American States. In the meantime, the United States gradually applied the remaining weapons in the arsenal of boycott. Moreover, the creation of the Alliance for Progress, announced before the invasion, was designed to check the spread of Castroism as well as to solve fundamental problems in Latin America. Some observers in the United States had, for a short while, a misplaced faith in the idea that the snow-balling economic problems in Cuba were the beginning of the end of Castro. United States' policy remained caught between the two extremes of accepting Castro and of taking direct action to eliminate him. Invariably official spokesmen fell back on the defense that ultimately military action would be taken if necessary. Within the confines of this essay, it is not possible to discuss this policy as an answer to Castro. But its effect upon the Russians was very clear. The attempt on the part of the United States to reassert control over the Cuban situation by gradual methods was regarded in Moscow as being evidence of

16

irresolution and faintheartedness on the part of America.

Although the Russians were struck by the seeming inde-
cision of American policy makers, Castro feared another
attack. He was by no means convinced that the United States
would not send another invasion force. This was the principal
reason he sought a more binding promise of Soviet aid than
that of "symbolic rockets." The Cubans sought to identify
themselves with the Russians in such a dramatic fashion that
the Soviet leaders would be virtually forced to take a more
forceful stand. President Dorticós during his visit to Russia
in September, 1961, announced in a way designed to flatter
and entrap the Russians: "We have entered the road of socialism."[34] In response, Russian spokesmen stressed the need to
make the tempo of Cuban economic development a showcase
for Latin America.[35] The final joint communiqué mentioned
Cuba's socialism only in passing.[36] To statements by the
Cubans that their country relied on Soviet offers of military
aid, the Russians answered that the support of "peace-loving
peoples" everywhere was Cuba's strongest defense.[37]

The next important step in defining Soviet-Cuban relations
was taken by Fidel Castro in his famous speech of December
2-3, 1961. In this lengthy and rambling discourse, he stated
that he was and always would be a Marxist-Leninist, and he
announced the impending formation of a one-party state.
This speech was the product of a complex of domestic and
foreign issues facing Castro. Its chief implication for foreign
affairs was revealed by his lavish praise of the Soviet Union
and the Cuban Communists, coupled with his open admission
of his conversion to communism. His statements, it appears,
were calculated to force the Soviets into making greater
economic and military investments in the Cuban revolu-

17

tion. Membership in the Warsaw Pact was probably again Castro's objective.

The Russian propaganda line on Cuba was wrecked by the Castro speech, especially so because the speech attracted wide attention and was often misinterpreted. The Russians now found it difficult to portray Cuba as mildly socialist at home and neutralist in foreign policy with the benevolent support of the Soviet Union. The earlier version of Castroism might have been reluctantly accepted by the United States, but an avowedly Marxist-Leninist Cuba might well be too much for the Americans to tolerate. A communist Cuba might also frighten nationalist and leftist supporters of Castroism in Latin America; and the collapse of a communist Cuba, already encountering severe economic difficulties, would represent a serious prestige defeat for the Kremlin.

The Soviets thus could not ignore the bearded liberator's profession of communist faith in December, 1961, as it had the milder claims of Dorticós the preceding September. But the Russians played it down.[38] Significantly, in the May, 1962, issue of the *World Marxist Review*, a long article appeared on the peaceful and non-peaceful paths to socialism. The essence of socialist revolution, it stated, was the creation of a socialist party by any means possible. The article contrasted the peaceful take-over in Czechoslovakia in 1948 and the violent revolution in China. The Cuban revolution was cited as evidence that the growth of Soviet power had in fact increased "the possibility of . . . socialist revolution being achieved by peaceful means." Even the Cubans, the article asserted, realized that their path of armed struggle was not the only way. Chile was spotlighted as a country in Latin America where peaceful means were feasible. Here, after World War II, the Communist Party was able to elect representatives to the national legislature and to establish a satisfactory alliance with the socialists. In Guatemala, Ecuador, and Peru on the other hand, the Cuban pattern was more likely the proper one. In effect, the article announced that the Cuban experience of armed rebellion should not be copied by all, certainly not by the more democratic, nations of Latin America.[39]

Though the Russians had accepted their self-proclaimed convert, they had apparently denied him any monopoly over communism in the Western Hemisphere. They also took great pains to deny a prevalent interpretation in the United States and Latin America that Castro in his speech of December 2-3 had proclaimed that he had been a Marxist-Leninist from the earliest days of the battle against Batista. Actually Castro had not said this, but in any case the Soviets went out of their way to deny the interpretation. Alexsey Adzhubey, Khrushchev's son-in-law, interviewed Castro, and the story was carried in the January 29, 1962, issue of *Pravda*. In the interview, Castro accused the imperialists of spreading the lie that the Cuban leaders had been Marxist-Leninists from the beginning and had consciously concealed their beliefs. He explained that, in the early stages of the revolution, he and his men were only revolutionaries drawn to socialism. By this means, the earlier Russian propaganda theme was in some small degree rescued from oblivion.[40]

The role of the Soviets in the crisis of March, 1962, in the Castro government is not entirely clear. The crisis became public knowledge when Castro told the faithful on March 26 that some of the "old communist militants" had misused their positions in the new collective leadership to commit sectarian crimes. Castro moved swiftly to purge many Cuban Communist Party stalwarts from the newly created unified political organization, but he also reiterated his devotion to Marxism-Leninism. The Russians signalled their approval by a story in their press defending Castro's action as consistent with the condemnation of sectarianism contained in the November, 1960, statement of the world's communist parties and later by calling for unity behind Fidel.[41] This was probably also a warning to the Cuban Communists to get in line. Commensurate with Cuba's new ideological position in the communist world, the May Day greetings for 1962 placed Cuba immediately after the European and Asian satellites and before Yugoslavia.[42] Even after this clear identification, the Soviet press on one occasion placed Cuba in the category of a non-socialist country, evidence of lingering doubt in Russian official circles about Castro's exact ideological status.[43]

The Soviet Union then accelerated her Cuban aid program early in 1962, subsidizing the Cuban economy for the first time. Soviet economic planners and technicians not only were more numerous and obvious than before but also began to exercise important influence over some aspects of the economy. Khrushchev showed Russian concern for Cuban economic conditions when he addressed Cuban students in Russia on the necessity for hard work, a message echoed in *Noticias de Hoy*, the Cuban communist paper, and, rather tardily, by Castro himself.[44] Also in the early part of 1962, a decision was reached to carry out a massive new military build-up in Cuba that went far beyond that of 1960. This culminated in the shipping of Russian missiles to Cuba. Although the deadtime needed for missile emplacement is not exactly known, the decision probably had to have been made no later than May or June, 1962, in order to get the missiles into Cuba by October, when they first arrived.

Reaction in the United States stressed the broader Cold War implications of this new Soviet move. Certainly the Russians had planned to utilize Cuba as an anchored missile ship. This would compensate for deficiencies in both land and submarine-based missiles and affect the balance of power. Certainly, too, the missiles were intended to influence the outcome of the forthcoming Berlin crisis. What has been too often overlooked is that Khrushchev by October, 1962, had deeply involved his country's power and prestige in the Cuban revolution. He took an obvious risk in sending missiles to Cuba, apparently with some degree of confidence. Since he knew the United States would soon discover the missiles, he must have believed there was more than an even chance that the United States would accept their presence. The Playa Girón invasion of April, 1961, was one reason for this miscalculation. In addition, if his gamble paid off, the missiles would have constituted additional insurance that the United States would coexist with a communist Cuba no matter how distasteful she might be. In a conversation with an American businessman during the crisis, Khrushchev remarked concerning Cuba, "You are not happy about it and you won't like it, but you'll learn to live with it." Keeping the missiles in the hands of Russian soldiers also served to give the Cubans some degree of confidence in the future without permitting irresponsible use of them. Moreover, it did not involve the Kremlin in a military alliance with Cuba. The large number of Soviet troops sent to Cuba with the missiles may have been intended, among other purposes, to give the Kremlin the military leverage it had applied so successfully on the governments of Eastern Europe. The Russian premier had good reason to believe that the Afro-Asians would regard the emplacement of the missiles as a legitimate action to help Cuba and that they would back him when, as he seems to have expected, the United States submitted the issue to the United Nations. After Khrushchev withdrew the missiles, he undoubtedly hoped to be regarded by the neutralists as a man of peace. The withdrawal of the missiles may seem from American shores like a complete victory, but it may not appear so elsewhere.

IV

Khrushchev feels a strong obligation to ensure the survival of Castroism. He and his predecessors had seldom, if ever, before dealt with a country that had voluntarily (that is, by choice of its leader) decided to become communist and an ally of the Soviet bloc. The normal Soviet method of exporting communism has been reliance upon military might to place and to support in power the local communist party. This was the case in the Balkans and in Eastern Europe. For the Russians, Cuba has emerged as something radically new and exciting but unpredictable. In their moments of exultation, the Soviets tend to believe that Castro's hasty swing to communism is a harbinger of new successes in Latin America. As an article in *Kommunist* stated in September, 1962, "it is not the mythical threat on the part of small Cuba but an entirely different reason that has unbalanced the American reactionaries; it is because the heroic revolutionary Cuba has firmly entered upon a new road and its example inspires fighters against North American imperialism in all of Latin America."[45] But in soberer moments, they see the difficulties inherent in backing a revolution so far distant and with so many problems.

The Soviets now have some important problems and related policy questions to decide. First, they must invest even more in Cuba to preserve the economic and political health of the Castro regime. This cannot be entirely a happy prospect, because the Soviets in Cuba will not be able to exercise the kind of direct military control they have used in Eastern Europe, at least if they withdraw their combat troops. In addition, Cuban economic needs may absorb a disproportionate part of Soviet foreign aid. If Russian technicians can get the sugar industry producing at pre-Castro levels, the Cubans may be able to pay for more of this aid, but this is a long-term problem.

A related question is the image of Castroism in the hemisphere. The reactions of the pro-Castro left demonstrate that the Latin Americans realize the Cold War is more directly and immediately a part of daily life in this hemisphere. The recent direct confrontation of the Soviet and United States power has forced the Latin Americans to re-evaluate the realities of power politics. The image of the Castro revolution as a truly Cuban social revolution has been so irreparably damaged that the Russians will be unable to restore it. And probably public opinion in Latin America has been polarized between the majority which now sees Castroism as a force of Soviet communism and the extremist minority which is so Communist-influenced that this revelation makes no difference. Some of the latter will insist upon the violent road à la Cuba and will receive some Chinese moral support.

The Russians very likely will place most of their money on
the non-violent road to communism.

1. Pedro Reyes, "Some Aspects of the Liberation Movement in Latin
America," *World Marxist Review*, II (January, 1959), 34-40.

2. *Pravda* (Moscow), November 18, 1959.

3. *New Times* (Moscow), No. 41 (October, 1959), pp. 17-18.

4. *Kommunist* (Moscow), October 15, 1959, p. 110. This issue lists Cuba
together with India, Indonesia, the U.A.R., Iraq, Burma, Sudan, Morocco,
Tunis, Ghana, and Guinea as countries which had become politically
independent.

5. *New Times*, No. 46 (November, 1960), p. 3.

6. *Current Digest of Soviet Press*, XI, No. 36, p. 16.

7. *New Times*, No. 33 (August, 1959), pp. 8-9; *New York Times*, December
5, 1959, p. 1.

8. Negotiations apparently began late in 1959 (*Pravda*, February 6, 7, 9,
10, 12, and 13, 1960).

9. *Izvestia*, February 16, 1960, p. 3; *New York Times*, February 15,
1960, p. 1.

10. To emphasize their alleged support for Castro from the first, the
Russians stressed that *de facto* relations had prevailed from January 1, 1959
(*New Times*, No. 21 [May, 1960], p. 9).

11. Russian spokesmen made the point that "only morbid minds can regard
Soviet-Cuban economic co-operation as a 'threat' to third powers" (Yuri
Bochkaryov, "Agreement with Cuba," *New Times*, No. 8 [February 8, 1960],
pp. 9-10). In a speech made in Oslo on his return from Cuba, Mikoyan took the
line that this was not a communist revolution but a national revolution caused
by exploitation, especially by capitalists from the United States. He deplored
news stories coming out of the United States that stated that he had gone to
Cuba to establish a "conspiracy" (*ibid.*, No. 9 [February, 1960], pp. 16-17).

12. According to an official Canadian report, Kudryavtsev was probably
the head of a Soviet spy ring in Canada (*New York Times*, July 8, 1960, p. 2.

13. *Ibid.*, May 9, 1960, p. 3.

14. The story is given in detail in Ronald M. Schneider, *Communism in
Guatemala 1944-1954* (New York, 1959).

15. K. Del Campo, "Lessons of the Revolution in Guatemala," *World
Marxist Review*, III (June, 1960), 31-37.

16. *Pravda*, June 6, 1960, p. 1.

17. *New York Times*, June 4, 1960, p. 1.

18. Henry Pachter, "The Meaning of Peaceful Coexistence," *Problems of
Communism*, X (1961), 1-8.

19. *Pravda*, October 14, 1960, p. 5; *ibid.*, October 21, 1960, p. 6.

20. In the United Nations, the U.S.S.R. backed the Cuban complaint of
United States aggression (*New York Times*, July 20, 1960, p. 4). A statement
on July 10 by TASS denied that Cuba was under the control of international
communism (*ibid.*, July 11, 1960, p. 6).

21. Khrushchev phrased his offer to help Cuba as an effort to assist a colonial people trying to break United States control rather than a communist or pro-communist regime (*ibid.*, July 10, 1960, p. 2; *ibid.*, October 29, 1960, p. 1; *ibid.*, October 30, 1960, p. 7; *Pravda*, November 12, 1960, p. 4).

22. Khrushchev said that if Communists were running the Cuban revolution, it would have proceeded in a different way. He denied that the Cuban leaders were Communists and compared his offer of military aid to that which the Soviet Union had given the Arab countries in the Suez crises. He also said that the United States was trying to interfere, as it had done in Guatemala in 1954, and that the Cuban case was a lesson for other colonial peoples (*New York Times*, July 13, 1960, p. 6). In a September interview with C. S. Sulzberger of the *New York Times*, Krushchev stated that Castro was not a Communist, but that he would be welcomed if he wished to join the Party (*ibid.*, September 8, 1961, p. 10).

23. Raúl Castro, minister of defense, visited Moscow on July 18, 1960, and in a speech on July 20 said that the Soviet Union had prevented the United States military intervention in Cuba (*ibid.*, July 21, 1960, p. 2; *ibid.*, July 22, 1960, p. 7).

24. *Ibid.*, June 10, 1961, p. 6.

25. The Soviets in July promised necessary economic aid to resist a blockade by the United States (*ibid.*, July 22, 1960, p. 7; *Pravda*, July 26, 1960, p. 1). Regarding the $50,000,000 worth of arms sent to Cuba, see the State Department pamphlet on Cuba quoted in *New York Times*, April 3, 1961, p. 14.

26. *Pravda*, December 20, 1960, p. 1.

27. *Ibid.*, August 31, 1960, p. 2; *International Affairs*, No. 11 (November, 1960), p. 22.

28. *New York Times*, No. 17 '(April, 1961), pp. 11-12.

29. *New York Times*, April 19, 1961, p. 1; *ibid.*, April 23, 1961, p. 1.

30. *Pravda*, May 3, 1961, p. 1.

31. *Pravda* carried detailed and extensive reports on United States reaction to the invasion failure. *Pravda*, on May 5, reported that James Reston's articles of April 30 and May 3 in the *New York Times* showed fear and chaos in Washington.

32. Vadim Zagladin, "Crushing Defeat for Exporters of Counter-Revolution: First Lessons of the Events in Cuba," *World Marxist Review*, IV (June, 1961), 50-56.

33. *New York Times*, August 15, 1961, p. 1; *Pravda*, May 8, 1961, p. 4.

34. *Pravda*, September 12, 1961, p. 1.

35. *Ibid.*, September 21, 1961, pp. 1, 23; September 22, 1961, editorial on p. 1.

36. *Ibid.*, September 21, 1961, pp. 1-2.

37. *Ibid.*, September 12, 1961, p. 2.

38. For an example, see *ibid.*, January 3, 1961, pp. 1, 4.

39. George Kar, "The Socialist Revolution—Peaceful and Non-Peaceful," *World Marxist Review*, V (May, 1962), 30-38.

40. *Pravda*, January 29, 1962, p. 3.

41. Speech quoted in *Pravda*, March 29, 1962, p. 4; April 11, 1962, p. 5. See also *ibid.*, June 15, 1962, p. 5.

42. *Ibid*, May 4, 1962, p. 1; April 15, 1962, p. 1.

43. *Ibid.*, May 10, 1962, p. 2.
44. *Ibid.*, June 3, 1962, pp. 1, 2.
45. *Kommunist*, September, 1962, p. 89.

THE ROLE OF THE INTELLECTUAL IN FOMENTING CHANGE: THE UNIVERSITY

JOHN P. HARRISON

TRADITIONALLY, the intellectual has been accorded a place of honor and respect in Hispanic American society. To be an intellectual is so important a qualification for popular acclaim in Latin America that those politicians whose situation demands popular support and who do not have the intellectual's qualifications invent them. The best-known recent example of one who felt such a need and whose invention proved quite successful was Juan Perón. The participation of intellectuals in the entourage of Mexican revolutionary leaders is well known; and in line with this thesis was the obvious attempt to extend the popularity and authority of Castro throughout Latin America by using continuously the title "Doctor" instead of "Fidel" in news and publicity releases during the first eighteen months after his descent from the Sierra Maestra.

A definition of the function and role of the intellectual is difficult in any society. In Latin America a few influential intellectuals like Octavio Paz can write: "Thinking is the first obligation of the intelligentsia, and in certain cases it is the only one."[1] But the objectivity and originality implicit in such a phrase do not characterize that body of Latin American intellectuals who today are marching—or milling, if one prefers—in the ideological faiths of communism, socialism, anti-imperialism, existentialism, or even in some instances, free enterprise. In this vein a sociologist has remarked: "The attenuation of the power of ideology is one of the positive signs of the sanity of the intellectual. But his strength also depends upon his willingness to refrain from being an ideologue—his willingness to be, in that sense, alienated." Other sociologists see the intellectual in terms of his occupation rather than his inner attitude, as one who creates or disseminates culture as part of his job. Still another view is that of the political scientist who believes that in order to qualify as an intellectual one has to concern himself with cultural symbols and abstractions outside his own professional field and, at the same time, must have sufficient integrity to know whether or not in any particular situation he is facing a compromise of an idea.[2]

While it is possible to accept all or part of these statements, they are not crucial in isolating that part of Latin American society which is playing an ideologically active role in contemporary politics. As within the present-day social and economic ferment in Latin America—"the blurred and shapeless face of the agrarian and nationalist revolution," as one of the more cosmopolitan Latin American intellectuals describes this phenomenon—so in this essay, the word *intellectual* will be confined to its operative use, viewed in terms

28

similar to those used by Edward Shils in describing Asian intellectuals. Shils defines the latter as all those with an advanced modern education.[3] In Latin America this definition must be extended to anyone within or graduated from an institution of higher education. The mere fact of being a student qualifies one as an intellectual with the right—extending to a duty—to inform and lead society as a whole. This particular sense of duty is in direct proportion to the extent one is an ardent nationalist; from the point of view of class structure, this militancy is strongest among those students from the lower and emergent middle class.

It has become commonplace in explaining some of the fundamental differences between the societies of the United States and Latin America to contrast the active role and glorified image of the intellectual in Latin America with the more modest status of his counterpart in the United States. Certainly it is difficult for intellectuals in the latter to conceive of a writer—and one frequently critical of the social values of his country—being accorded the massive obeisance paid the Chilean poetess Gabriela Mistral when her body arrived in Santiago for final interment. The respect paid to intellectuals in Hispanic society has not, however, improved their economic position or assured their honest and fair treatment in the market place. Gabriela Mistral, to use her as an example a second time, encountered great difficulty in collecting royalties from her Chilean publishers while she was living abroad. A moderately strong tradition exists, however, by which the state awards government positions to outstanding writers. These might, in some instances, be regarded as sinecures, but the intellectuals are being paid essentially for political services and are not being rewarded directly as teachers or writers. Those *pensadores* who serve their country, such as Alfonso Reyes, Daniel Cosió Villegas, or Octavio Paz to use but three of many Mexican examples, do an exceedingly competent job advancing the political interests of their government both at home and abroad.

While their numbers are slowly increasing, very few intellectuals in Latin America are able to maintain themselves from the income derived from their writings, from their salaries as university professors, or from research activities. The only reasonably sure way to advance both their ideas and their personal well-being has been through politics. There is no connotation of "second choice" in this process, for the Latin American usually regards the highest expression of his intellectual efforts to be their effect on national and continental politics. The natural corollary of this is that he seeks the political opportunity, a launching platform so to speak, to make his contributions to society. This is a forum devoutly and consistently sought after by all intellectuals. It would be interesting to select twenty outstanding Latin Americans from among those who have made major intellectual contributions who have remained essentially within an intellectual or academic sphere. The percentage that first attempted the direct route of politics and failed could then be determined. In other words, one might discover those who were rejected from the active political arena and were, so to speak, relegated to its margin to carry on purely intellectual pursuits.

A characteristic of Latin American intellectuals, distinguishing them from their counterparts elsewhere in the Western world, is the extent to which their emphasis on social thought impels them toward an active political life or, at the very least, toward an effort to influence social decisions through political means. That during the nineteenth and the early twentieth century those who wrote and taught were inadequately paid for this function was not significant, because the intellectuals were part of a small upper class which supported its writers and teachers by means other than direct payment. After World War I, the restrictions on entrance into the university were sufficiently removed to permit a proportionately vast increase in the number of those who considered themselves intellectuals—many of them from families without wealth or connections. While economic and social questions have traditionally been a matter of concern for Latin American intellectuals, it was only with the emergence of intellectuals such as José Carlos Mariátegui, the author of the influential *Seven Essays Interpreting the Realities of Peruvian Life* (1928), from the lower— certainly poorer—strata of society that the basic values of the existing social structure were seriously questioned.

The availability of a university education to the growing middle class of Latin America was made possible by the University Reform Movement that exploded in the Río de la Plata during the second decade of this century—an explosion that had a rapid if uneven fallout north to the Río Bravo. The Latin American university in 1918 was an integral part of an essentially static social structure. It was an effective institution that contributed to the traditional elite's ability to maintain control over society. The elite was able both to limit the number of those entering the university and—a second check—to restrict the granting of degrees to those who matriculated. The University Reform Movement was sufficiently strong to change the educational institutions which had previously supported the *ancien régime* in Latin America. Through the fissures brought about by the Reform have seeped, and at times poured, those students who have provided the intellectual attack on the entrenched social and economic interests that have dominated politics in Latin America since the wars of independence.

It is essential to realize that while the University Reform Movement cracked the existing structure of higher education, and in secondary schools to a lesser degree, it by no means brought about a collapse of the old system. Its success varied greatly in both time and place throughout the hemisphere. The partial nature of their gains has caused those students and faculty members supporting the Reform to continue placing the primary emphasis on the aspects of the Movement directed toward a redefinition of the national and, ultimately, continental conscience. This helps explain the student emphasis today, as forty years ago, on certain features of the Reform. They oppose any academic limitations to matriculation other than graduation from a secondary school; they demand both the right to repeat courses as often as may be necessary to pass and periodic checks on a professor's competence in order to prevent the holder of a chair from supporting the interests of the "oligarchy." Among other things, they insist on examinations which are open to review as the only basis for passing or failing a student and on student participation in university administration to insure implementation of their program. All of these features are designed to make the individual opportunity and collective advantages of higher education available to all classes of society, but most specifically, to that group referred to as the upwardly mobile or emerging middle class.

The necessity of placing continual emphasis on the essentially political question of making higher education available to the lower sectors of society, with their belief in the need of social and political reform, has prevented any serious concern over certain critical academic matters. The University Reform Movement has paid no attention to the quality of teaching, the rigor and nature of instruction, or any academically substantive question. This is true despite the fact that the *reforma universitaria* has been the longest continual expression of the revolution of social and economic aspirations generally assumed to be sweeping Latin America. Already at least two generations of politically active and socially motivated students have emerged as the most vocal members of the Latin American intelligentsia, yet they do not have the specialized professional training needed to meet the productive and technical needs of an increasingly industrialized society. In part, this explains the position taken by many student leaders—particularly those in the larger national universities—who believe there is no reason to devote attention to academic reform until political reform is achieved. This, of course, shows no confidence in the political structure and social values of the government in power, a position taken recently by 90 per cent of the students at the National University in Bogotá. Supporting data, if not so conclusive, are available on student attitudes in other countries.

Juxtaposed with the enormous political consciousness among university students is the political attitude of the submerged masses of the urban and rural poor who are supposed to provide the eruptive force within Latin America's "revolution of rising expectations." The results of the recent sparse, and geographically widely separated, empirical studies of these attitudes by United States social scientists such as Daniel Goldrich indicate that the possibilities are against any sweeping, region-wide social revolution despite population pressures, unproductive economies, and ineffective governments. While the potential for basic changes is greater today than previously, Goldrich remarks: " . . . The awesome and more general truth about submerged peoples everywhere is the amount of misery they can accept without revolt. Under conditions of extreme poverty and continued inability to ameliorate it, people are as likely to become socially disorganized as to be impelled into political action. . . ."[4] Recent surveys have revealed, among other things, that only approximately 6 per cent of the population in rural São Paulo could identify Fidel Castro; that the urban and rural poor in Latin America do not seriously *expect* their government to do anything to alleviate the situation; that only 20 per cent of the *favelados* of Rio de Janeiro had engaged a friend in serious political discussion in the previous six months; that one in fifty from rural areas, from among those who had been sufficiently active in the Arbenz regime to have been jailed for a period of time after his overthrow, could identify Karl Marx, and one in eight John Foster Dulles, despite the fact that the former secretary of state had been featured on the anti–United States posters plastered about the large rural landholdings of Guatemala.

It is possible, however, to give a different interpretation as to what may be expected from the conjunction of the politically inert urban and rural poor with the large percentage of young intellectuals who are totally alienated from the values and political processes of the existing political administration and who are seeking a radical reconstruction of society. Since this vocal group of intellectuals is totally unprepared to meet the specialized technical demands for increasing the productive capacity of their nation, they are seeking purely political answers to immense economic and social problems. Their training and their attitudes give them no other recourse than to appeal in ever more stringent ideological terms and an ever more strident demagogic manner to the residents of Latin America's rapidly growing urban shack slums. There is no generic Spanish word to describe this relatively recent phenomenon in Latin America. *Callampa, favela, barreada, villa de miseria,* or simply *colonia* indicate a well-defined area of crowded living quarters with few if any community services, inhabited by people who normally do not have legal title to the land, who often pay no rent, and who originally came from rural areas.

The possibility of an alliance of university intellectuals with the urban poor is increased by the primacy of capital cities in Latin America and the location of national universities—the natural habitat of the upwardly mobile lower-middle class—in the capital cities. The results of this alliance, which appears to be a highly probable eventuality, will depend in large part on (1) the extent to which there is a well-directed and disciplined cadre of communists to plan and to lead; (2) the extent to which other universities have produced both intellectuals and socially oriented technicians who are demonstrably improving the productive capacity of the nation in ratio to its population; and (3) whether the existing government has a sufficiently organized political machine to enable it (a) to carry out any democratic mandate it may have and (b) to counter—with force, if necessary—the overwhelming Hispanic respect for the university as the source for social ideology and the fount of plans for its political implementation.

The same kind of alliance between intellectuals and impoverished city dwellers may also develop in larger provincial cities wherever a state university has existed for a substantial period of time, at least antedating World War II. In these areas both the strength of regional feelings, as opposed to nationalism, and the size and newness of the shack slum will determine the strength of the ties between political *universitarios* and urban poor.

In Latin America the university student considers himself an intellectual and is so accepted by a society in which the overwhelming majority of intellectuals are politically oriented and seek their goals almost solely through political means. Politically active students, especially those in national universities, are more concerned with the restructuring of society than in finding solutions to the immediate and localized problems of economic and social development which concern their national governments. They are, in a very real sense, still fighting the *ancien régime*—something the intellectual of the left in the United States has never had to do. Their opposition is negative. The intellectuals constitute groups or individuals who refuse in principle to consider the problems of the government as real tasks needing resolution. They oppose the existing order without any constructive position of their own on specific issues, even in their own institutions. A group of student leaders in Colombia at one time informed the writer that curriculum and administrative changes within the university would come only after all vestiges of the old social order had been swept away. Given this point of view, they will not consider action in support of educationally purposeful programs.

One can postulate, then, that if student organizations continue to be successful in stopping or even in substantially slowing down the national universities' efforts at academic reform in the interests of over-all economic and social development, the graduates of private universities, supplemented by some foreign-trained students, will, short of political revolution, gain a monopoly over the principal decision-making positions in and out of government.[5] This would mean that the national universities would be shunted to a secondary position similar to that which normal schools have traditionally occupied in the United States. It would mean also that the transmission of culture, described by Ortega y Gasset as the primary function of a university, would, by default, be passed into the hands of the very social class against whom the proponents of the *reforma universitaria* have been struggling for nearly half a century.

It is difficult to believe, however, that any largely centralized government in Latin America would allow its national university to sink to a position where it does not provide at least a substantial part of the elite or the political decision-making sector of society. If the national university does not participate in setting the tone and the goals for higher education, a centralized government engaged in responsible national planning will experience difficulty in achieving its goals and presumably will lose part of its control over the kind of human product in which it is investing.

Middle-class students in the national and larger state universities perceive this situation. They believe, however, that private universities are being supported by those who wish to encourage an educational system conducive to the retention of influence and power by the present or old elite groups. This feeling is responsible for opposition to academic reforms in the national university which would limit access to a free university education and make it more difficult to obtain a degree, the symbol which raises the student's status and that of his family within the social structure. These academic and curricular reforms are, of course, precisely the ones needed to provide the specialized skills necessary for effective national development. The loss of prestige in higher education by a national university is most noticeable in Colombia. Continual disruption of the academic program at major national universities by student political activities is most notorious in Venezuela and Peru. One result of constant student pressures at the University of San Marcos in Lima has been to encourage the previously specialized national universities of engineering and agronomy to develop coursework in the biological and physical sciences, humanities, and social sciences—much in the pattern of the United States land-grant colleges. There can be no doubt that the struggle now going on within the national universities between the totally alienated student groups supporting the Reform and those working for more rigorous training to meet national needs for economic development and to provide a broader social access to its products may well be decisive in determining the future political form of Latin American nations.

This statement is not a gross exaggeration; one must remember that Latin America "accepts the proposition that the political ideologies of a society should be developed in a university."[6] In the process of providing for the economic and social needs of an expanding population, a choice will have to be made between a totalitarian government and democracy, between communism and a respect for individual human integrity. An essential part of this choice is that those forces working for social change within a non-totalitarian context must be able to meet the demands of an accelerating technology with resources they control and with a self-generated energy. Both the development of these skills and the intellectual training that supports their cultivation will have to come from the university. Such a program has to have a broad base of support within the ambitious and aggressive politically active group now gaining access to higher social status and to the national political decision-making machinery. Both skills and attitudes must be developed to a considerable degree within the national and larger state universities. These politically active intellectuals believe in state planning, and they want the educative process in the hands of the state, for only in this way will they have a voice in the planning process. If the national university does not prepare the human capital needed for economic development, there will remain a permanent and debilitating distrust of solutions that create serious obstacles to the mobility of the new middle class. Such a condition would provide a seductive theme that could be played with infinite variations by that relatively small number of well-organized students supported by an equally well-oriented number of writers and other intellectuals outside of the university who are committed to total political revolution as the only solution to the social and economic problems of Latin America. If this latter group can prevent the development of an educational system that provides the varied specialists needed for material development — agricultural and industrial—the ultimate answer to meeting the needs of the rural and urban poor will be a new version of the Cuban or Yenan way.

The weapons available to those intellectuals in favor of total change, and by this very fact opposed to the gradual nature of academic reform, are considerable. They are addressing a society where any student is accepted as an intellectual without yet having met the Western world's standard of an intellectual's ability to use concepts or carry on a dialogue. It is possible, of course, that one can renounce argument and resort to force somewhat in the same way an artist can draw figures but resorts to abstraction. The problem of the new intellectual is that he resorts to ideology without having mastered the arguments or exhausted the dialogue, in reality, without ever having become engaged. For the student and nearly all intellectuals, social questions or moral judgments take precedence over economic and social factors, and are more easily comprehended. The committed intellectual with a system in his pocket is in an advantageous position to influence the Latin American who, to emancipate himself from old forms, must be a member of some authoritative congenial collectivity. The preference of Latin Americans for moral criticism brings them easily into a position of no compromise. Similarly, their feeling for mystical qualities makes it easier than in other cultures to endow a word such as *proletariat* with a mystique quite incomprehensible to most North Americans. (One way, incidentally, to acquire a visual image of this mystique is to read the program notes and to see a university-student production of a Brecht play staged in a workers' *barrio*.) In this same vein, Raymond Aron has observed that "the resurrection, in a seemingly scientific form, has a natural appeal for minds weaned on faith."[7] The messiah presented by the ideologue signifies a break with the past; and the United States, for many Latin Americans, is closely associated with the past from which they want to break. Likewise, Aron's remark about intellectuals being more pained than ordinary mortals by the hegemony of the United States can be italicized for Latin America. The extension of this hegemony to the field of higher education by the introduction of academic reforms, which many consider to be a North American import, is especially unpalatable to an intellectual.

This incomplete analysis has explained in part why the new intellectuals in Latin America condemn all academic reforms that would improve the quality of university training. They see them as attempts to prolong the life of an odious system. Such a feeling is heightened by the fact that intellectuals have been directly affected by oppression and poverty to which the intellectual everywhere is so keenly sensitive. Francisco Miró Quesada, a sophisticated Peruvian intellectual, points out that because students come from both the middle class and from the working class, they are, as intellectuals, peculiarly conscious of the meaning of the class struggle. But "as both litigant and judge, as members of an exploited class and an institution with higher political status, they [have] lost sight of the concept of the university and reduced it to a purely political role, to an ideological battlefield."[8] The crucial issue is to extricate the universities from this predicament so that their students may meet the human needs of their society with the necessary specialized tools for national development, while at the same time performing the continuing university function of transmitting culture and generating new definitions of traditional values. This is the central problem that the intellectual of Latin America must answer. And it is one that the *reformista universitario* in his effort at reforming society from above has failed to resolve: either in changing society or in producing a university in the modern sense of the word, i.e., a center of cultural creation and a center for the training and research of specialists.

1. Octavio Paz, *The Labyrinth of Solitude: Life and Thought in Mexico*, trans. Lysander Kemp (New York, 1961), p. 192.

2. For various views on the role and function of the intellectual see Seymour M. Lipset *et al.*, "American Intellectuals: Their Politics and Status," *Daedalus*, LXXXVIII (Summer, 1959), 460-98.

3. Edward Shils, *The Intellectuals in the Political Development of the New States* (Stanford, Calif.: Center for Advanced Study in the Behavioral Sciences, n. d.), p. 8. Shils comments that this definition will become increasingly inadequate as the number of Asians and Africans with an advanced, specialized education increases.

4. Daniel Goldrich, "Toward an Estimate of the Probability of Social Revolutions in Latin America: Some Orienting Concepts and a Case Study," *The Centennial Review of Arts and Sciences*, V (1962), 395.

5. In Latin America, "private university" signifies any non-state university and, consequently, for most Latin Americans the term means only a Catholic university despite the fact that a few excellent private, non-denominational universities do exist. The argument can be made that because Catholic universities emphasize the traditional and professional aspects of culture rather than science and technology, there is scant prospect of their fulfilling the educational needs of economic and social development.

6. Francisco Miró Quesada, "The University South and North: The University and Society," *Américas*, XII (December, 1960), 3.

7. Raymond Aron, *The Opium of the Intellectuals*, trans. Terence Kilmartin (London, 1957), p. 66.

8. Miró Quesada, *op. cit.*, p. 5.

THE FORCE
OF THE
CHURCH

JOHN J. KENNEDY

DURING World War II, it was reported that the late Joseph Stalin dismissed the possibility of consultation between Allied leaders and the Papacy with the cynical question: "The Pope—how many divisions does he command?" In strictly military terms, of course, the question required no answer. Questions about the force of the Church are, however, normally stated in other terms, and the answers may reflect a wide variety of interests. The theologian offers answers of one kind; the canonist, of another, the doctrinal apologist of still another; while the historian of religion may present something quite different from all the others. To duplicate here the answers of any or all of these specialists would be pretentious. Rather what is assumed to be at issue is the question of the social power of the Catholic church in Latin America; an assessment of that power in terms meaningful to students of politics and international relations will be undertaken here.

A fundamental preliminary in this evaluation is some rudimentary identification of the nature of the Church in Latin America. One body of opinion, too extensive and too erudite to be dismissed lightly, has seen the Latin American Church as an anachronistic survival of organized superstition in an age of reason and enlightenment.[1] In another view, the Church is essentially an instrument used by the economic and social elite to control and, on occasion, to oppress the masses. Another characterization has won increasing popularity of late, especially in the United States. In this view the Latin American Church can be regarded, hopefully, as a mighty, if cumbersome, weapon against international communism, which not only threatens social elites in Latin America but is also a great nuisance to North America. None of these characterizations, however, is of much help for present purposes. They do less to explain the force of the Church than they do to explain it away.

The best possibilities for analysis probably lie in regarding Catholicism simply as a religion that commands the loyalty of large numbers of human beings who live under widely diverse conditions and who are committed to a creed which seeks to account for man in the universe. The creed, moreover, provides for a Church that claims the authority to define and apply the principles of the creed itself in order to present man with the opportunity to gain salvation, not in this world, but in eternity. All of this may seem rather elementary. It is; but if it were not for these elements of belief, commitment, and authority, the Church would present no problem — at least no basic problem — to students of politics.

The problem begins to take shape with the consideration that, if the goals of the Catholic religion are not of this world, the Catholic church has rarely hesitated to involve itself in the affairs of this world. Involvement has generally been on one of the two following bases: (1) In this world the Church must be assured of an unhampered sphere of action for the fulfilment of its mission. While the Church will not insist that this sphere be everywhere and always uniformly defined, it will zealously seek to keep the area of operation one of its own choice and definition and will resist any efforts of other parties to establish its limits. The church-state conflicts, which fill so large a part of the modern history of the West, have in last analysis frequently turned on this point. These conflicts have resulted in various kinds of resistance on the Church's part. Its general attitude, however, was stated by Pope Leo XIII who emphasized that as the Church pursues "by far the noblest of ends, so is its authority the most exalted of all authority, nor can it be looked upon as inferior to the civil power, or in any way dependent upon it."[2] (2) If human life has its goal in eternity, the conditions of life in this world should be consistent with that goal and conducive to it. The conditions are primarily to be determined by the integrity and dignity of mankind and the individual. The Church may not claim of itself competence to create these conditions or the responsibility for maintaining them, but it will, again and again, insist on a self-defined right to inspire and influence the course of events that may produce them.

There is a temptation to say that the history of the Church in republican Latin America can be told in terms of selection and rejection between these two bases. In the first century after independence, the Church acted largely on the first; now emphasis is being shifted to the second. This idea has the attractiveness of simplicity and would seem to suggest an explanation of the apparent difference in behavior on the part of churchmen in the two periods. The one appears to be marked by the prevalence of church-state tensions arising from the efforts of churchmen to keep the sphere of ecclesiastical activity one of their own choice. The other is distinguished chiefly by the social concerns of the Church.

This, however, is too simple a view. It involves an assumption that the pattern of church-state relations is no longer a serious question for the Church—or for the State—an assumption which is not generally warranted. This is not to deny that there are signs of a shift in emphasis, but the evidence suggests other factors to be investigated before attributing change to abandonment of a traditional position. The increasingly urbanized character of Latin American society obviously presents to the Church a different complex of problems from that which a predominantly agricultural society once produced. The Latin American Church existed for centuries in a society where communities were isolated one from the other. This separation determined in part the basic patterns of ecclesiastical activity. Isolation has not everywhere vanished, but its force has been broken to a considerable extent by the appearance of technological factors in society, such as radio communications and mechanized transportation. These and a myriad of related factors have obviously modified the task of the Church. In examining specific modifications in its general task, however, one should bear in mind that the basic interests of the Church do not change.

All that has been laid down so far has been in terms of the general and the ideal. Reality has on occasion marred the ideal. Certain churchmen in Latin America, as elsewhere, have demonstrated more zeal for temporal concerns than for the eternal. Others have abused their authority. Moreover, the record of bad performance has not been limited to the ranks of the ordained. Conspicuous violation of principles of the Catholic laity has not been entirely unknown in Latin America.

In attempting to evaluate the social force of the Church in Latin America, one must acknowledge this divergence between the ideal and the real, but it is also necessary to recognize two related considerations. One is that the long-range significance of the Church has to be found in terms of the ideal. The other is that the gap between the ideal and the real is often a narrow one and sometimes non-existent. Appraisal also requires recognition of what has been suggested above, namely, that if the Church faces a changing task in an evolving society, the concern and interests that the Church pursues are permanent and unchanging. Against the background of these considerations it is pertinent to evaluate the Church today within the scope outlined by the three following categories: (1) the current state of civil-ecclesiastical relations; (2) Church influences on social change; (3) some consequences of the factors considered under the above two headings for the position of Latin America in world affairs, especially within the inter-American system.

In connection with the first, there seems to be a new public image of the Latin American Church. Feature writers in newspapers and pictorial magazines give North Americans the impression of a new progressive Church whose leaders are anxious to scrape the barnacles off the old vessel and render her shiningly new and modern. This attitude means, among other things, that the new Church will assign secondary importance, or even less, to the question of how the state regards the Church. The suggestion is that the Church is no longer genuinely concerned about whether it has an official position, a recognized position, a neutral position, or whether its position is a matter of indifference to public authority. The further suggestion is that the happy day of complete separation of church and state is about to dawn, and no group will greet this news more eagerly than North American Catholics who have found the attitudes of their co-religionists in Latin America incomprehensible, not to say embarrassing, on this point as on so many others.

Eagerness along these lines had best be restrained. It will largely meet with disappointment. Separation of church and state in the North American fashion is not possible for most of Latin America in the forseeable future. The use of the North American model can only continue to provide, as it has in the past, a misleading standard for comparison. It is true that legal separation has been constitutionally established in many countries: in Mexico, nearly a century ago; in Brazil and Cuba, with the advent of the republic; and in Chile and Uruguay, more than a generation ago. In few, if any, of these countries, however, does the situation resemble that in the United States. Church and state have parted company, but they have often been unable to go their separate ways. Religious issues survive in politics. Conflicts occur, and occasionally they are bitter, as in Mexico in the 1920's. This is not to suggest that the conflicts can be resolved by reverting to the pre-separation status, a most unrealistic consideration. What is important is the acknowledgment that separation has not necessarily eliminated conflict.

But, it can be asked, is the situation any more disadvantageous for society in the foregoing countries than it is in the countries where the two authorities have not had separate courses assigned but where their overlapping interests and jurisdictions are frankly acknowledged? Examples are found in Colombia, where the acknowledgment is made through a concordat, or in Argentina, where it is made through constitutional stipulation. Have not these two countries been the scene of more political-religious tension in the past two decades than Mexico or Chile? The answer to this question, however, must take into account the survival of regalism in most countries where church and state are not completely separated. Moreover, the spirit of regalism may be re-enforced by that of nationalism which gives rise to suspicions of the "foreign" or cosmopolitan character of a universal Church. In the name of nationalism the state may seek guarantees that control of the Church be placed in the hands of its own citizens, as the Colombian government sought and obtained in the 1942 revision of the Concordat. In general, in countries with a strongly asserted regalistic tradition, the central question of Church patronage appears to be one that neither side desires to raise in any drastic or final way. Indeed, in Argentina each party seems to wish to meet the other half-way in the maintenance of that curious camouflage that always surrounds the exercise of patronal claims.[3]

Certain dedicated Catholics have been known to argue that the whole regalistic arrangement imposes so many liabilities on their Church that sacrifice of official status would be a small price to pay for getting rid of the arrangement.[4] The argument has so far failed to persuade the various national hierarchies, who apparently prefer to suffer disadvantages they have learned to live with than to risk experimentation. Even if Church authorities could bring themselves to accept the hypothesis, there would, however, remain the problem of convincing the civil authorities. In most countries of the regalistic tradition, the latter task would probably prove harder than the former.

This whole problem of church-state relations would certainly be different if Latin America possessed a genuine diversity of creeds and churches. While there has been a notable expansion of Protestant groups in certain countries in recent years, the development is not yet of a proportion to provide a new perspective for the church-state picture.

In summary, the church-state problem in Latin America continues. It is too firmly emplanted in the inheritance of the area to be eliminated in a generation or two. It is evident both in the tensions that appear from time to time and in the accommodations between the two parties. New social attitudes in the Church may mean that new and different accommodations will be forthcoming; but it is difficult, if not impossible, to envisage any arrangements that will isolate church and state, one from the other.

Within the second category of evaluation, Church influence on social change, general interest seems to center on the question of what role the Latin American Church will play in the future that it has not played in the past. At the present time this question will probably produce more speculation than definitive answers.

It is reasonable for speculation along these lines to anticipate some innovations on the part of the Church. It would, however, be quite unreasonable to expect any influence or support from the Church that would run counter to well-established orthodoxy in doctrine or practice.

This may appear a superfluous affirmation, but it is stressed because certain original and creative personalities within the Latin American Church have sometimes been regarded, at least in the United States, as being in fundamental disagreement with their fellows. Bishop Miguel de Andrea in Argentina or Father Alberto Hurtado in Chile are good examples. Andrea, especially, is often presented as though he had spent his life in a continual battle against other bishops. Then, when it is argued that men of his kind speak for the future of the Church, the implication is that in the future the Church will put less stress on orthodoxy. Bishop Andrea undoubtedly had a keener sensitivity to social trends than many other churchmen. This sensitivity made him a champion of social reform, and it is for this reason that his name has importance. But one has only to dip into his religious writings to realize that the bishop was not only orthodox but even conventional in his piety.[5] His work indicates that vigorous support of social reform is possible from the Church, but there is nothing in it to suggest that such support involves a departure from orthodoxy.

A second consideration is that while the Church seems to take a generally sympathetic regard for social legislation—and this regard indicates support for measures dealing with land reform, labor conditions, public housing, and public health—the Church cannot be evaluated solely as a militant social reform organization. The Church has an advantage in

51

this connection because it can appeal to the conscience of the believer in terms of social obligation. It is significant that for many Latin Americans the Church is the most effective channel of appeal to provoke the desired response. But not all Latin Americans are believers. Non-believers bent on social reform may welcome the support of the Church. Collaboration of this sort is not entirely new or unprecedented. Twenty years ago in Argentina, Bishop Andrea and the Socialist leader Alfredo Palacios could both endorse, within the confines of a single book, certain advancements in labor legislation.[6] In such collaboration, however, each party has its own basis for action, and these bases will not necessarily be identical. By and large, the difference between them need not produce any great problems, but there is a possibility that in certain areas it may.

In terms of its own doctrinal interests, the Church is especially sensitive in the areas of the creation and maintenance of the family and in the education of youth. Here, conflicts are possible, even probable, in certain cases. In present circumstances it probably can be assumed that there will be a search for various ways to resolve such conflicts, but there should be no expectation that the Church will retreat from its doctrinal positions. There would seem to be a promise of minimizing conflict, however, if the Church could be persuaded to take one genuinely innovating step. This move would be the frank recognition of the presence of numerous unbelievers in Latin American societies. Too often, churchmen seem to be the prisoners of their own statistics. The national census reports that about 98 per cent of the population of a particular country in Latin America is Catholic; in reality only 20 to 30 per cent may be active

Church members. Churchmen are keenly aware of the difference, but they have long demonstrated a reluctance to admit it, and this reluctance has sometimes led them into difficult, not to say unrealistic, attitudes toward public policy. In defense of these same churchmen, it can be pleaded that their awareness extends also to other matters that must be considered here. Foremost among them is the fact that the 98 per cent figure does represent the baptized, and, generally speaking, those baptized in the Church are to be regarded as members of the Church unless by deed or word they specifically separate themselves. To limit pastoral responsibility to the 20 to 30 per cent of practicing Catholics is to attribute to the Church an exclusiveness which is incompatible with both its purpose and its history.

It does not involve any challenge to pastoral responsibility, however, to point out that the 20 to 30 per cent are responsive to pastoral authority in a way that the others are not. To ask ecclesiastical authorities to recognize this fact and to take account of it in their plans and work is not to ask the Church to sacrifice any doctrine. Nor is it to suggest that the Church be restrained in its efforts to expand the number of practicing members. Open acknowledgment of the fact that not all Latin Americans are practicing Catholics could, however, be an important step in creating an atmosphere where the Church's legitimate interest in social reform could be exercised in conjunction with other reform interests with a minimum of conflict.

If the possibility of conflict deserves some attention, it is no less important to note that in many parts of Latin America, tradition supports the concept of a working harmony between the Church and various elements in society. It is an oversimplification to say that in the past this harmony was dependent upon a political party, generally a conservative one, on the one side and the Church hierarchy on the other. Nevertheless, it is true that in certain countries, notably Chile and Colombia, the Conservative party was popularly regarded as the Church party, although elsewhere, notably Argentina, the conservatives were not so identified. By and large, however, the identity of Catholic with the conservative seems to be disappearing. At the same time, new political parties have emerged under the general designation of Christian Democracy, and the designation itself is an indication of, at the very least, strong sympathy with values the Church has sought to uphold.

For the student of Latin American government and politics, the obvious question is this: In the future, will an identity between Catholic and Christian Democrat be established as there was in the past between Conservative and Catholic? A definitive answer is probably not possible at this time, but the indications are to the contrary. Christian Democratic leaders generally profess a personal adherence to the Church, but so do leaders of other groups. Christian Democratic leaders claim the social doctrine of the Church as their particular source of inspiration, but they emphasize the absence of any organizational connection between their parties and the Church. In most countries the movements are of relatively recent origin, and it may be too early to undertake an appraisal of their impact. Their ideological commitments, however, suggest that traditional Christian teachings are adaptable to new situations, and in this connection the movements may reflect the abiding force of the Church.

Another significant facet of this general topic requires a

fighters against North American imperialism in all of Latin America."[45] But in soberer moments, they see the difficulties inherent in backing a revolution so far distant and with so many problems.

The Soviets now have some important problems and related policy questions to decide. First, they must invest even more in Cuba to preserve the economic and political health of the Castro regime. This cannot be entirely a happy prospect, because the Soviets in Cuba will not be able to exercise the kind of direct military control they have used in Eastern Europe, at least if they withdraw their combat troops. In addition, Cuban economic needs may absorb a disproportionate part of Soviet foreign aid. If Russian technicians can get the sugar industry producing at pre-Castro levels, the Cubans may be able to pay for more of this aid, but this is a long-term problem.

A related question is the image of Castroism in the hemisphere. The reactions of the pro-Castro left demonstrate that the Latin Americans realize the Cold War is more directly and immediately a part of daily life in this hemisphere. The recent direct confrontation of the Soviet and United States power has forced the Latin Americans to re-evaluate the realities of power politics. The image of the Castro revolution as a truly Cuban social revolution has been so irreparably damaged that the Russians will be unable to restore it. And probably public opinion in Latin America has been polarized between the majority which now sees Castroism as a force of Soviet communism and the extremist minority which is so Communist-influenced that this revelation makes no difference. Some of the latter will insist upon the violent road à la Cuba and will receive some Chinese moral support.

23

The Russians very likely will place most of their money on the non-violent road to communism.

1. Pedro Reyes, "Some Aspects of the Liberation Movement in Latin America," *World Marxist Review*, II (January, 1959), 34-40.

2. *Pravda* (Moscow), November 18, 1959.

3. *New Times* (Moscow), No. 41 (October, 1959), pp. 17-18.

4. *Kommunist* (Moscow), October 15, 1959, p. 110. This issue lists Cuba together with India, Indonesia, the U.A.R., Iraq, Burma, Sudan, Morocco, Tunis, Ghana, and Guinea as countries which had become politically independent.

5. *New Times*, No. 46 (November, 1960), p. 3.

6. *Current Digest of Soviet Press*, XI, No. 36, p. 16.

7. *New Times*, No. 33 (August, 1959), pp. 8-9; *New York Times*, December 5, 1959, p. 1.

8. Negotiations apparently began late in 1959 (*Pravda*, February 6, 7, 9, 10, 12, and 13, 1960).

9. *Izvestia*, February 16, 1960, p. 3; *New York Times*, February 15, 1960, p. 1.

10. To emphasize their alleged support for Castro from the first, the Russians stressed that *de facto* relations had prevailed from January 1, 1959 (*New Times*, No. 21 [May, 1960], p. 9).

11. Russian spokesmen made the point that "only morbid minds can regard Soviet-Cuban economic co-operation as a 'threat' to third powers" (Yuri Bochkaryov, "Agreement with Cuba," *New Times*, No. 8 [February 8, 1960], pp. 9-10). In a speech made in Oslo on his return from Cuba, Mikoyan took the line that this was not a communist revolution but a national revolution caused by exploitation, especially by capitalists from the United States. He deplored news stories coming out of the United States that stated that he had gone to Cuba to establish a "conspiracy" (*ibid.*, No. 9 [February, 1960], pp. 16-17).

12. According to an official Canadian report, Kudryavtsev was probably the head of a Soviet spy ring in Canada (*New York Times*, July 8, 1960, p. 2.

13. *Ibid.*, May 9, 1960, p. 3.

14. The story is given in detail in Ronald M. Schneider, *Communism in Guatemala 1944-1954* (New York, 1959).

15. K. Del Campo, "Lessons of the Revolution in Guatemala," *World Marxist Review*, III (June, 1960), 31-37.

16. *Pravda*, June 6, 1960, p. 1.

17. *New York Times*, June 4, 1960, p. 1.

18. Henry Pachter, "The Meaning of Peaceful Coexistence," *Problems of Communism*, X (1961), 1-8.

19. *Pravda*, October 14, 1960, p. 5; *ibid.*, October 21, 1960, p. 6.

20. In the United Nations, the U.S.S.R. backed the Cuban complaint of United States aggression (*New York Times*, July 20, 1960, p. 4). A statement on July 10 by TASS denied that Cuba was under the control of international communism (*ibid.*, July 11, 1960, p. 6).

21. Khrushchev phrased his offer to help Cuba as an effort to assist a colonial people trying to break United States control rather than a communist or pro-communist regime (*ibid.*, July 10, 1960, p. 2; *ibid.*, October 29, 1960, p. 1; *ibid.*, October 30, 1960, p. 7; *Pravda,* November 12, 1960, p. 4).

22. Khrushchev said that if Communists were running the Cuban revolution, it would have proceeded in a different way. He denied that the Cuban leaders were Communists and compared his offer of military aid to that which the Soviet Union had given the Arab countries in the Suez crises. He also said that the United States was trying to interfere, as it had done in Guatemala in 1954, and that the Cuban case was a lesson for other colonial peoples (*New York Times,* July 13, 1960, p. 6). In a September interview with C. S. Sulzberger of the *New York Times,* Krushchev stated that Castro was not a Communist, but that he would be welcomed if he wished to join the Party (*ibid.*, September 8, 1961, p. 10).

23. Raúl Castro, minister of defense, visited Moscow on July 18, 1960, and in a speech on July 20 said that the Soviet Union had prevented the United States military intervention in Cuba (*ibid.*, July 21, 1960, p. 2; *ibid.*, July 22, 1960, p. 7).

24. *Ibid.*, June 10, 1961, p. 6.

25. The Soviets in July promised necessary economic aid to resist a blockade by the United States (*ibid.*, July 22, 1960, p. 7; *Pravda,* July 26, 1960, p. 1). Regarding the $50,000,000 worth of arms sent to Cuba, see the State Department pamphlet on Cuba quoted in *New York Times,* April 3, 1961, p. 14.

26. *Pravda,* December 20, 1960, p. 1.

27. *Ibid.*, August 31, 1960, p. 2; *International Affairs,* No. 11 (November, 1960), p. 22.

28. *New York Times,* No. 17 (April, 1961), pp. 11-12.

29. *New York Times,* April 19, 1961, p. 1; *ibid.*, April 23, 1961, p. 1.

30. *Pravda,* May 3, 1961, p. 1.

31. *Pravda* carried detailed and extensive reports on United States reaction to the invasion failure. *Pravda,* on May 5, reported that James Reston's articles of April 30 and May 3 in the *New York Times* showed fear and chaos in Washington.

32. Vadim Zagladin, "Crushing Defeat for Exporters of Counter-Revolution: First Lessons of the Events in Cuba," *World Marxist Review,* IV (June, 1961), 50-56.

33. *New York Times,* August 15, 1961, p. 1; *Pravda,* May 8, 1961, p. 4.

34. *Pravda,* September 12, 1961, p. 1.

35. *Ibid.*, September 21, 1961, pp. 1, 23; September 22, 1961, editorial on p. 1.

36. *Ibid.*, September 21, 1961, pp. 1-2.

37. *Ibid.*, September 12, 1961, p. 2.

38. For an example, see *ibid.*, January 3, 1961, pp. 1, 4.

39. George Kar, "The Socialist Revolution—Peaceful and Non-Peaceful," *World Marxist Review,* V (May, 1962), 30-38.

40. *Pravda,* January 29, 1962, p. 3.

41. Speech quoted in *Pravda,* March 29, 1962, p. 4; April 11, 1962, p. 5. See also *ibid.*, June 15, 1962, p. 5.

42. *Ibid,* May 4, 1962, p. 1; April 15, 1962, p. 1.

43. *Ibid.*, May 10, 1962, p. 2.
44. *Ibid.*, June 3, 1962, pp. 1, 2.
45. *Kommunist,* September, 1962, p. 89.

THE ROLE OF THE
INTELLECTUAL
IN FOMENTING CHANGE:
THE UNIVERSITY

JOHN P. HARRISON

TRADITIONALLY, the intellectual has been accorded a place of honor and respect in Hispanic American society. To be an intellectual is so important a qualification for popular acclaim in Latin America that those politicians whose situation demands popular support and who do not have the intellectual's qualifications invent them. The best-known recent example of one who felt such a need and whose invention proved quite successful was Juan Perón. The participation of intellectuals in the entourage of Mexican revolutionary leaders is well known; and in line with this thesis was the obvious attempt to extend the popularity and authority of Castro throughout Latin America by using continuously the title "Doctor" instead of "Fidel" in news and publicity releases during the first eighteen months after his descent from the Sierra Maestra.

A definition of the function and role of the intellectual is

27

difficult in any society. In Latin America a few influential intellectuals like Octavio Paz can write: "Thinking is the first obligation of the intelligentsia, and in certain cases it is the only one."[1] But the objectivity and originality implicit in such a phrase do not characterize that body of Latin American intellectuals who today are marching—or milling, if one prefers—in the ideological faiths of communism, socialism, anti-imperialism, existentialism, or even in some instances, free enterprise. In this vein a sociologist has remarked: "The attenuation of the power of ideology is one of the positive signs of the sanity of the intellectual. But his strength also depends upon his willingness to refrain from being an ideologue—his willingness to be, in that sense, alienated." Other sociologists see the intellectual in terms of his occupation rather than his inner attitude, as one who creates or disseminates culture as part of his job. Still another view is that of the political scientist who believes that in order to qualify as an intellectual one has to concern himself with cultural symbols and abstractions outside his own professional field and, at the same time, must have sufficient integrity to know whether or not in any particular situation he is facing a compromise of an idea.[2]

While it is possible to accept all or part of these statements, they are not crucial in isolating that part of Latin American society which is playing an ideologically active role in contemporary politics. As within the present-day social and economic ferment in Latin America—"the blurred and shapeless face of the agrarian and nationalist revolution," as one of the more cosmopolitan Latin American intellectuals describes this phenomenon—so in this essay, the word *intellectual* will be confined to its operative use, viewed in terms

28

similar to those used by Edward Shils in describing Asian intellectuals. Shils defines the latter as all those with an advanced modern education.[3] In Latin America this definition must be extended to anyone within or graduated from an institution of higher education. The mere fact of being a student qualifies one as an intellectual with the right— extending to a duty—to inform and lead society as a whole. This particular sense of duty is in direct proportion to the extent one is an ardent nationalist; from the point of view of class structure, this militancy is strongest among those students from the lower and emergent middle class.

It has become commonplace in explaining some of the fundamental differences between the societies of the United States and Latin America to contrast the active role and glorified image of the intellectual in Latin America with the more modest status of his counterpart in the United States. Certainly it is difficult for intellectuals in the latter to conceive of a writer—and one frequently critical of the social values of his country—being accorded the massive obeisance paid the Chilean poetess Gabriela Mistral when her body arrived in Santiago for final interment. The respect paid to intellectuals in Hispanic society has not, however, improved their economic position or assured their honest and fair treatment in the market place. Gabriela Mistral, to use her as an example a second time, encountered great difficulty in collecting royalties from her Chilean publishers while she was living abroad. A moderately strong tradition exists, however, by which the state awards government positions to outstanding writers. These might, in some instances, be regarded as sinecures, but the intellectuals are being paid essentially for political services and are not being

29

rewarded directly as teachers or writers. Those *pensadores* who serve their country, such as Alfonso Reyes, Daniel Cosió Villegas, or Octavio Paz to use but three of many Mexican examples, do an exceedingly competent job advancing the political interests of their government both at home and abroad.

While their numbers are slowly increasing, very few intellectuals in Latin America are able to maintain themselves from the income derived from their writings, from their salaries as university professors, or from research activities. The only reasonably sure way to advance both their ideas and their personal well-being has been through politics. There is no connotation of "second choice" in this process, for the Latin American usually regards the highest expression of his intellectual efforts to be their effect on national and continental politics. The natural corollary of this is that he seeks the political opportunity, a launching platform so to speak, to make his contributions to society. This is a forum devoutly and consistently sought after by all intellectuals. It would be interesting to select twenty outstanding Latin Americans from among those who have made major intellectual contributions who have remained essentially within an intellectual or academic sphere. The percentage that first attempted the direct route of politics and failed could then be determined. In other words, one might discover those who were rejected from the active political arena and were, so to speak, relegated to its margin to carry on purely intellectual pursuits.

A characteristic of Latin American intellectuals, distinguishing them from their counterparts elsewhere in the Western world, is the extent to which their emphasis on social thought impels them toward an active political life or, at the very least, toward an effort to influence social decisions through political means. That during the nineteenth and the early twentieth century those who wrote and taught were inadequately paid for this function was not significant, because the intellectuals were part of a small upper class which supported its writers and teachers by means other than direct payment. After World War I, the restrictions on entrance into the university were sufficiently removed to permit a proportionately vast increase in the number of those who considered themselves intellectuals—many of them from families without wealth or connections. While economic and social questions have traditionally been a matter of concern for Latin American intellectuals, it was only with the emergence of intellectuals such as José Carlos Mariátegui, the author of the influential *Seven Essays Interpreting the Realities of Peruvian Life* (1928), from the lower—certainly poorer—strata of society that the basic values of the existing social structure were seriously questioned.

The availability of a university education to the growing middle class of Latin America was made possible by the University Reform Movement that exploded in the Río de la Plata during the second decade of this century—an explosion that had a rapid if uneven fallout north to the Río Bravo. The Latin American university in 1918 was an integral part of an essentially static social structure. It was an effective institution that contributed to the traditional elite's ability to maintain control over society. The elite was able both to limit the number of those entering the university and—a second check—to restrict the granting of degrees to those who matriculated. The University Reform Movement was sufficiently strong to change the educational institutions which had previously supported the *ancien régime* in Latin America. Through the fissures brought about by the Reform have seeped, and at times poured, those students who have provided the intellectual attack on the entrenched social and economic interests that have dominated politics in Latin America since the wars of independence.

It is essential to realize that while the University Reform Movement cracked the existing structure of higher education, and in secondary schools to a lesser degree, it by no means brought about a collapse of the old system. Its success varied greatly in both time and place throughout the hemisphere. The partial nature of their gains has caused those students and faculty members supporting the Reform to continue placing the primary emphasis on the aspects of the Movement directed toward a redefinition of the national and, ultimately, continental conscience. This helps explain the student emphasis today, as forty years ago, on certain features of the Reform. They oppose any academic limitations to matriculation other than graduation from a secondary school; they demand both the right to repeat courses as often as may be necessary to pass and periodic checks on a professor's competence in order to prevent the holder of a chair from supporting the interests of the "oligarchy." Among other things, they insist on examinations which are open to review as the only basis for passing or failing a student and on student participation in university administration to insure implementation of their program. All of these features are designed to make the individual opportunity and collective advantages of higher education available to all classes of society, but most specifically, to that group referred to as the upwardly mobile or emerging middle class.

The necessity of placing continual emphasis on the essentially political question of making higher education available to the lower sectors of society, with their belief in the need of social and political reform, has prevented any serious concern over certain critical academic matters. The University Reform Movement has paid no attention to the quality of teaching, the rigor and nature of instruction, or any academically substantive question. This is true despite the fact that the *reforma universitaria* has been the longest continual expression of the revolution of social and economic aspirations generally assumed to be sweeping Latin America. Already at least two generations of politically active and socially motivated students have emerged as the most vocal members of the Latin American intelligentsia, yet they do not have the specialized professional training needed to meet the productive and technical needs of an increasingly industrialized society. In part, this explains the position taken by many student leaders—particularly those in the larger national universities—who believe there is no reason to devote attention to academic reform until political reform is achieved. This, of course, shows no confidence in the political structure and social values of the government in power, a position taken recently by 90 per cent of the students at the National University in Bogotá. Supporting data, if not so conclusive, are available on student attitudes in other countries.

Juxtaposed with the enormous political consciousness among university students is the political attitude of the submerged masses of the urban and rural poor who are supposed to provide the eruptive force within Latin America's "revolution of rising expectations." The results of the recent sparse, and geographically widely separated, empirical studies of these attitudes by United States social scientists such as Daniel Goldrich indicate that the possibilities are against any sweeping, region-wide social revolution despite population pressures, unproductive economies, and ineffective governments. While the potential for basic changes is greater today than previously, Goldrich remarks: " . . . The awesome and more general truth about submerged peoples everywhere is the amount of misery they can accept without revolt. Under conditions of extreme poverty and continued inability to ameliorate it, people are as likely to become socially disorganized as to be impelled into political action. . . ."[4] Recent surveys have revealed, among other things, that only approximately 6 per cent of the population in rural São Paulo could identify Fidel Castro; that the urban and rural poor in Latin America do not seriously *expect* their government to do anything to alleviate the situation; that only 20 per cent of the *favelados* of Rio de Janeiro had engaged a friend in serious political discussion in the previous six months; that one in fifty from rural areas, from among those who had been sufficiently active in the Arbenz regime to have been jailed for a period of time after his overthrow, could identify Karl Marx, and one in eight John Foster Dulles, despite the fact that the former secretary of state had been featured on the anti–United States posters plastered about the large rural landholdings of Guatemala.

It is possible, however, to give a different interpretation as to what may be expected from the conjunction of the politically inert urban and rural poor with the large percentage of young intellectuals who are totally alienated from the values and political processes of the existing political administration and who are seeking a radical reconstruction of society. Since this vocal group of intellectuals is totally unprepared to meet the specialized technical demands for increasing the productive capacity of their nation, they are seeking purely political answers to immense economic and social problems. Their training and their attitudes give them no other recourse than to appeal in ever more stringent ideological terms and an ever more strident demagogic manner to the residents of Latin America's rapidly growing urban shack slums. There is no generic Spanish word to describe this relatively recent phenomenon in Latin America. *Callampa, favela, barreada, villa de miseria,* or simply *colonia* indicate a well-defined area of crowded living quarters with few if any community services, inhabited by people who normally do not have legal title to the land, who often pay no rent, and who originally came from rural areas.

The possibility of an alliance of university intellectuals with the urban poor is increased by the primacy of capital cities in Latin America and the location of national universities—the natural habitat of the upwardly mobile lower-middle class—in the capital cities. The results of this alliance, which appears to be a highly probable eventuality, will depend in large part on (1) the extent to which there is a well-directed and disciplined cadre of communists to plan and to lead; (2) the extent to which other universities have produced both intellectuals and socially oriented technicians who are demonstrably improving the productive capacity of the nation in ratio to its population; and (3) whether the existing government has a sufficiently organized political machine to enable it (a) to carry out any democratic mandate it may have and (b) to counter—with force, if necessary—the overwhelming Hispanic respect for the university as the source for social ideology and the fount of plans for its political implementation.

The same kind of alliance between intellectuals and impoverished city dwellers may also develop in larger provincial cities wherever a state university has existed for a substantial period of time, at least antedating World War II. In these areas both the strength of regional feelings, as opposed to nationalism, and the size and newness of the shack slum will determine the strength of the ties between political *universitarios* and urban poor.

In Latin America the university student considers himself an intellectual and is so accepted by a society in which the overwhelming majority of intellectuals are politically oriented and seek their goals almost solely through political means. Politically active students, especially those in national universities, are more concerned with the restructuring of society than in finding solutions to the immediate and localized problems of economic and social development which concern their national governments. They are, in a very real sense, still fighting the *ancien régime*—something the intellectual of the left in the United States has never had to do. Their opposition is negative. The intellectuals constitute groups or individuals who refuse in principle to consider the problems of the government as real tasks needing resolution. They oppose the existing order without any constructive position of their own on specific issues, even in their own institutions. A group of student leaders in Colombia at one time informed the writer that curriculum and administrative changes within the university would come only after all vestiges of the old social order had been swept away. Given this point of view, they will not consider action in support of educationally purposeful programs.

One can postulate, then, that if student organizations continue to be successful in stopping or even in substantially slowing down the national universities' efforts at academic reform in the interests of over-all economic and social development, the graduates of private universities, supplemented by some foreign-trained students, will, short of political revolution, gain a monopoly over the principal decision-making positions in and out of government.[5] This would mean that the national universities would be shunted to a secondary position similar to that which normal schools have traditionally occupied in the United States. It would mean also that the transmission of culture, described by Ortega y Gasset as the primary function of a university, would, by default, be passed into the hands of the very social class against whom the proponents of the *reforma universitaria* have been struggling for nearly half a century.

It is difficult to believe, however, that any largely centralized government in Latin America would allow its national university to sink to a position where it does not provide at least a substantial part of the elite or the political decision-making sector of society. If the national university does not participate in setting the tone and the goals for higher education, a centralized government engaged in responsible national planning will experience difficulty in achieving its goals and presumably will lose part of its control over the kind of human product in which it is investing.

Middle-class students in the national and larger state universities perceive this situation. They believe, however, that private universities are being supported by those who wish to encourage an educational system conducive to the retention of influence and power by the present or old elite groups. This feeling is responsible for opposition to academic reforms in the national university which would limit access to a free university education and make it more difficult to obtain a degree, the symbol which raises the student's status and that of his family within the social structure. These academic and curricular reforms are, of course, precisely the ones needed to provide the specialized skills necessary for effective national development. The loss of prestige in higher education by a national university is most noticeable in Colombia. Continual disruption of the academic program at major national universities by student political activities is most notorious in Venezuela and Peru. One result of constant student pressures at the University of San Marcos in Lima has been to encourage the previously specialized national universities of engineering and agronomy to develop coursework in the biological and physical sciences, humanities, and social sciences—much in the pattern of the United States land-grant colleges. There can be no doubt that the struggle now going on within the national universities between the totally alienated student groups supporting the Reform and those working for more rigorous training to meet national needs for economic development and to provide a broader social access to its products may well be decisive in determining the future political form of Latin American nations.

This statement is not a gross exaggeration; one must re-

upper-group, oligarchic rulers and new aspirants for power. As a result of this socio-political crisis in 1930, the military once more re-entered the political arena in force. After having left the scene for more than half a century, they now returned to moderate the social crisis. At first, some army officers appeared on the scene as advocates of change, and in many countries the oligarchs willingly vacated the presidential palaces in favor of army officers. Most of the oligarchs, it appeared, counted on conservative generals to use force to preserve the traditional order from threats of change from the left.

Though often differing in timing, the trends were remarkably similar in so many countries that it is possible to discuss a general pattern and relationship between the role of the military and the developing social crisis. The span of thirty-two years following the onset of the great depression may be divided into three main periods: (1) a period (1930-1943) of unrest, coups, and countercoups, and generally unsuccessful challenges to the old social order; (2) a decade (1943-1953) of revolt against the old order and social reform, marked in some cases by the appearance of a new civilian leadership and in others by a new kind of military dictator, of which Juan Perón was the prototype; and (3) a period of reaction and counterrevolution marked by a slowing or halting of the pace of social reform, a trend reinforced by the events of the Cuban upheaval. This third period, extending roughly from 1947 to the present, overlaps the previous period because the tide of social revolution began to recede in some countries before it had reached its crest in others. In many cases elements of the armed forces engaged on each side of the struggle.

71

When the great depression struck, rightist military dictators were already in power in Cuba and Venezuela. During the years 1930-1931, seven more dictatorial regimes appeared—in Argentina, Peru, Ecuador, Bolivia, El Salvador, the Dominican Republic, and Guatemala. An increasingly conservative general, Plutarco Elias Calles, ran political affairs in Mexico, and United States marines controlled Nicaragua and Haiti. Indeed, the influence of the military had become so pervasive in the early 1930's that civilian governments existed in only three countries—Uruguay, Costa Rica, and Colombia.

Not all military influence was directed toward the support of conservatism. The revolts in Brazil in 1930, Panama in 1931, and Cuba in 1933 brought to the fore military elements that were more attentive to the demands of previously neglected middle- and low-income groups. After the destructive Chaco War, successful, but short-lived, revolts occurred in both Paraguay and Bolivia during 1936 under the leadership of radical young officers inspired by ideas of social reform and authoritarian nationalism.

On the eve of World War II, however, the political picture in Latin America had generally reverted to the rightist authoritarian pattern. The brief flurry of military-led political radicalism that had appeared in a few Latin American countries had spent itself. When war broke out in Europe in 1939, conservative generals ran twelve of the twenty republics while traditionalists regimes, maintained in office by the armed forces, controlled three other countries. Chile, Costa Rica, Uruguay, Colombia, and Mexico were the only countries where the armed forces did not play key conservative socio-political roles.

The effect of World War II upon Latin American politics was to freeze traditionalist regimes in power. The wartime emergency provided dictatorial regimes with justification for outlawing political experimentation and major social or economic reform for the duration. The United States, whose overriding consideration was strategic, also did her best to maintain stability in Latin America, sought the co-operation of incumbent regimes which were willing to help the war effort, and provided them with military and economic aid.

Yet the war produced pressures that made maintenance of the status quo increasingly difficult. The outbreak of hostilities in Europe seriously disturbed the economy of Latin America. Shortages of manufactured goods and foodstuffs were common because of the lack of transportation. The sudden interruption of imports from the United States and from Europe thus gave a great impetus to industrialization in Latin America, a trend stimulated by financial assistance from the United States. Despite wartime shortages of labor and equipment, Latin America's industrial establishment grew by leaps and bounds.

Wartime prosperity, however, had no broad base. Governments froze wages, prohibited strikes, and even outlawed labor movements in some countries. Hardships suffered by middle- and lower-income groups intensified social stresses and strains. It became merely a matter of time before popular pressures would again break through the dikes, bringing in a flood of political and social changes.

The decade 1943-1953 was, in general, one of revolt against the old order. Civilian foes of the status quo were joined by military ones, mostly young officers restless under a static armed forces organization that offered little opportunity for change and advancement. In the latter years of World War II, an assortment of disgruntled, patriotic, ambitious colonels and majors began joining rising popular movements. As a result, a cycle of revolutions occurred in Latin America far more fundamental than the palace revolts of the past.

The first breakthrough was the seizure of power in Argentina by Colonel Juan Perón and his colleagues in 1943. A new revolt in Bolivia later in that year was both an echo of events in Buenos Aires and a recrudescence of the junior-officer radical movement of the 1930's. The influence of *Peronismo* spread further northward in the next decade, affecting many countries of the Caribbean and Central America.

Meanwhile, other, more democratic influences were making themselves felt. With the fall of totalitarian dictatorship in Italy and its impending destruction in Germany and Japan, authoritarian regimes, even some of the more progressive ones, were discredited. In 1944, traditionalist governments were overthrown in Ecuador and in Guatemala by popular revolutions led by young officers. Batista's power as *de facto* ruler of Cuba disappeared when his candidate lost to a popular coalition in the 1944 elections. In 1945, Vargas was forced to step down in Brazil because of a combination of army prodding and popular pressures. In the same year, popular reform-minded parties came to power in both Venezuela (with military assistance) and Peru. Later manifestations of the same trend were the revolutions of 1948 in El Salvador and Costa Rica, and of 1952 in Panama. The profound social upheaval that took place in Bolivia in 1952 and the Colombian army's coup, which ousted the extreme right-wing regime of Laureano Gómez in 1953, also seemed to presage a new era of economic and social advancement.

Colombia's revolution ended Latin America's post-war cycle of popular reform, generally through violent change. Twelve Latin American nations, containing 75 per cent of the population of that area, experienced varying degrees of progress between 1943 and 1953. Five minor countries (Dominican Republic, Nicaragua, Paraguay, Haiti, and Honduras) did not. Reform-minded regimes already held power in Mexico, Chile, and Uruguay; but in these countries, the political role of the armed forces was not a determining factor.

By 1953, the cycle of revolution and reform had already been overlapped by a new cycle of counterrevolution. As early as 1947, when the wave of social change seemed to be carrying all of Latin America before it, political currents in some countries began flowing in the opposite direction. Sensing the threat of demagoguery, violence, and extremism, rising middle-class groups and many army officers lost some of their enthusiasm for reform. Older, traditionalist groups seized opportunities to reassert themselves. The reaction thus generated continued unabated for an entire decade until every government of the reformist type had either been overturned or forced to adopt a more moderate course.

In 1948 the seizure of power by Colonel Marcos Pérez Jiménez in Venezuela and by General Manuel Odría in Peru marked the beginning of the drift back to the right. The effects of El Salvador's revolution of 1948 evaporated within a few years. Both Haiti and Cuba felt the sting of resurgent rightist militarism in 1950 and 1952, respectively.

In Guatemala the revolt of 1954, which saved the country from the communists, restored much of the old order. In Brazil, Vargas' apparent scorn for constitutional limitations and his emulation of Perón in demagogic appeals to the masses led the army to force his resignation in 1954. In 1955 came the assassination of Colonel José Antonio Remón in Panama and the fall of Perón. This was followed two years later by the demise of Colombia's reform-minded strong man, General Gustavo Rojas Pinilla. In all these cases the dictator was succeeded by a regime largely representative of the traditional ruling groups.

The armed forces played a leading role in this trend to the right. Usually, at the behest of either the oligarchy or the frightened middle class, the army stepped in to halt further leftward evolution. Reformist rulers often lost a measure of popular support because of their methods or because of their failure to fulfil demagogic promises. Yet the people did not desert them or withdraw their support of the regime. What generally happened was that the military intervened either when they themselves or when civilian groups which had won their support were sufficiently provoked by the new leaders' actions such as softness towards organized labor, deliberate efforts to widen existing social cleavages, or irresponsible, undemocratic, or totalitarian methods of government. Often the military found themselves unmaking the very revolutions they themselves had sponsored several years previously.

III

When the entire picture is examined, both historical and

76

contemporary, it is difficult to escape the conclusion that the armed forces represent a force for continuity rather than for change. The immediate post–World War II years, when the military in many countries prompted reform, are an exception, almost an aberration, in the Latin American historical experience. On the balance, the armed forces have been a force for preservation of the status quo; their political intervention has generally signified, as it does today, a conservative action, even to the point of dissolving popular political parties by force.

Even in those few cases in the past when the military were in the vanguard of the forces of change, their leaders nearly always perverted or distorted the original aims of the revolution. Reform-minded military leaders generally came to power with a majority of the people behind them. For a short time, they drew upon a reservoir of popular support, launched ambitious projects for economic development, and enacted social-welfare measures. Yet, somehow, these regimes became more totalitarian and eventually stopped their drive for reform. It appeared at times as though the new military rulers were psychologically unprepared to accept authentically popular solutions to their national problems.

The record shows that the military leader's ardor for reform generally cools rapidly in the aftermath of victory, slowing any program of social advancement. Also, victors inevitably demand spoils, and the enrichment of the new military elite, including the reform-minded dictator, soon makes his government appear to the populace more and more like that of its exploiting predecessors. The dictator's mounting problems are complicated by his political incompetence and his often ill-conceived, ruinous economic policies. All this gives new courage to the traditionalist opposition, who are joined by many who had supported the liberal revolution. Faced with mounting resistance, the dictator tightens control and increases his repressive measures in a desperate attempt to hold power. Ultimately, the armed forces split. When that occurs, the days of the dictator are numbered.

Such was the fate, in a general way, of Ibañez in Chile, in 1931; of Villaroel in Bolivia, in 1946; of Arbenz in Guatemala, in 1954; of Perón in Argentina, in 1955; and of Rojas Pinilla in Colombia, in 1957. Neither they nor their military colleagues had the ability or the determination to solve their national problems in an orderly progressive fashion. Latin America is still looking for its first truly competent reform-minded strong man.

The picture of the static, retrogressive role of the military in Latin America today is indeed a bleak one; but all hope should not be lost, for there are at least a few positive indicators on the horizon. One of the more promising is the assumption by some military organizations of an extra-military function which seems far more wholesome for them than politics. This is the Civic Action program, now being promoted by the United States government. Civic Action merely means that the military will contribute their technical expertise to assist the nation in fostering social and economic progress, promoting industrialization, developing communications and public works projects, starting agricultural colonies in remote areas, providing health services, building hospitals and schools, and co-operating in anti-illiteracy campaigns. This is an old concept, utilized sporadically in Mexico, Brazil, Cuba, Argentina, Peru, Chile, and Bolivia since the 1930's. But what is new is the growing magnitude of the

78

effort. The program is just getting under way, and it remains to be seen to what degree the military will accept a useful and constructive non-military responsibility.

Finally, it is a much too gloomy prospect to assume that the military will hew stubbornly to their present penchant for continuity until such time as they are all destroyed in a violent popular upheaval such as those which have occurred in Mexico, Bolivia, and Cuba. Certainly, some officers in the armed services today are thinking in terms of alternatives. The pendulum between military and civilian rule and between reaction and reform has swung in the past and will swing again in the future. The military must eventually begin to relent on their stubborn refusal to allow popularly elected reform governments to come to power. Both the Brazilian and Argentine military appear to be wavering on this issue at present, and it is not inconceivable that the Peruvian military will yet find a way of doing business with the Apristas.

If in some countries civilian government cannot prevail, it is still possible that truly competent military strong men will emerge to offer progressive leadership to various Latin American countries. A Latin American army may yet produce a Nasir or perhaps even a Mustafa Kemal Atatürk, and this might be a most hopeful sign in view of the current unwillingness of the military to allow civilian reform regimes to operate in some countries.

1. A January, 1963, plebiscite restored the Presidential system of government.

LAND REFORM AS AN EXPLOSIVE FORCE IN LATIN AMERICA*

THOMAS F. CARROLL

"THE AGITATION must come from below. From you and from all your brothers. Shouting and marching. Down with the latifundio! Down with tyranny! Long live land reform! Long live liberty! All the ears will be listening to the crowd. You are the crowd. And the heart of the latifundio which is of stone will melt away, like ice. Because the clamor of the masses has the heat of fire. . . ."[1]

This is the voice of Francisco Julião, organizer of the Peasant Leagues in the poverty-stricken northeast of Brazil. Such voices are heard with increasing frequency in a continent where the agrarian problem, long a forbidden and subversive topic, has jumped to sudden prominence and even respectability. Agitation, unrest, violence, which have become

*The author gratefully acknowledges the aid of Clyde Mitchell and Lowry Nelson who read the manuscript and supplied critical comments.

characteristic of the sprawling urban areas are now spreading to the hitherto more passive countryside. Yet, among the explosive forces operating in Latin America perhaps none is more controversial and hotly argued than land reform. While the discussion of land reform has become fashionable for public debate and for serious policy consideration in the best circles, the controversy over the problem still persists, even intensifies. Tensions and conflicts over land multiply. For all of the current debate, land reform remains a most elusive and multifaceted concept. The purpose of this paper is not so much to analyze the arguments for and against land reform, nor to propose the most appropriate types of reforms to deal with the various kinds of agrarian maladjustments, but to explain why land reform is considered such a burning issue in Latin America and to sketch the main reasons why it is an explosive force.[2] (The term "explosive force" is interpreted as something responsible for great social tension and instability, conducive to violent or drastic action by large groups of people, as distinguished from routine activities or isolated actions by individuals).

At the heart of the land-reform problem in most Latin American countries is the unsatisfactory land-tenure situation, persisting stubbornly as a semi-feudal or seignorial agrarian structure inherited from colonial times. It is easy to list the main manifestations of this agrarian heritage: the *latifundia-minifundia* pattern of land holding, a rural class society sharply divided into masters and quasi-serfs (frequently accentuated by ethnic stratification), forms of peonage, onerous tenancy, insecurity, lack of mobility, and generally low levels of human development. It is not so much that rural people are poor—poverty is their lot almost everywhere—but that in Latin America this poverty coexists with a concentration of wealth and, curiously enough, with a relative abundance of natural resources. It is this inequality, this imbalance along with the well-known inflexibility, that is causing the land-tenure system to be blamed as one of the main obstacles to development in Latin America. Land reforms—large-scale changes in the land-tenure system plus other institutional changes—are increasingly regarded, therefore, as a prerequisite to accelerated growth or development.

What makes these reforms so controversial is that they invariably involve a drastic re-ordering of property relationships and thereby a redistribution of power. Thus, land reforms, if they are at all meaningful in scope and intensity, are, by their very nature, revolutionary changes. The recognition of this inherent "explosiveness" in land reform seems difficult for evolution-minded Americans. It is hoped that needed changes can be accomplished gradually, within the established legal framework and without undue sacrifice of order and political stability and without damage to the going economy. This may be an illusion. Land reform, in situations of rigidity, where the land-tenure system has not undergone gradual modification, cannot be a series of small neatly adjusted changes, but must be a head-on attack on the status quo. Thus, land reform in the Latin American setting is not an adjustment to market freedom, or an "unfreezing of the factors of production" as liberal economists desire. It becomes rather the embodiment of essential contradiction to the established market and legal relations in which price, access to resources, markets, and even justice are functions of the extreme concentration of property and power. This means quite simply a change in the "rules of the game," rather than a better strategy to make the participants more competitive. J. Kenneth Galbraith, perhaps one of the spiritual originators of the Alliance for Progress, expresses this clearly when he writes:

> Unfortunately, some of our current discussion of land reform in the underdeveloped countries proceeds as though this reform were something that a government proclaims on any fine morning—that it gives land to tenants as it might reform the administration of justice. In fact, a land reform is a revolutionary step; it passes power, property and status from one group in the community to another. If the government of the country is dominated or strongly influenced by the land-holding groups —the one that is losing its prerogatives—no one should expect effective land legislation as an act of grace. . . .[3]

At this stage of events in Latin America, one seems faced with the dilemma that land reform, when seriously undertaken, is an explosive and unpredictable business, but may be much more explosive when left undone. It will be argued that rural tensions are likely to intensify as conditions of income and social justice continue to stagnate or to decline while the perception to the possibility of change increases. An attempt will be made to show that a certain amount of violence, unrest, and disorder is unavoidable and even necessary for successful reform measures, the initiation of which is likely to create further disturbing or unsettling elements. A clearer realization of this unpleasant probability and a realistic assessment of the alternatives (which may only admit various kinds of violent situations) would go a long way toward clarifying the aims of United States policy and strengthening the thrust of both material and psychological action programs.

Intellectual Pressures

One must first consider the current intellectual environment which supplies much of the motivation and justification for radical tenure changes. Intellectually speaking, there are two main lines of argument or reasoning for drastic land reform: first, a rapid modification of the land-holding system is deemed necessary in order to speed up farm production and to modernize agriculture; second, a thorough overhauling of the land system is regarded as a prerequisite to achieve a measure of social justice and to attain a better distribution of rights and opportunities in line with current aspirations. These twin pressures for land reforms appear in various admixtures in all discussions. They provide the leitmotifs of leading Latin American thinkers who, even in non-Marxist circles, increasingly preclude a "gradualistic" or indirect approach. Although it is neither possible nor often desirable to make a rigid separation between what may be called the economic and the socio-political aspects of land reform, any analysis of this question must be approached from these two major contexts.

PRODUCTIVE EFFICIENCY

The prevailing land-tenure system is believed to be a major cause for chronic stagnation of Latin American agriculture. That farm production in the region is inefficient needs little demonstration. Almost 60 per cent of the population of Latin America is still rural, while the contribution of the farm sector to the gross national product is below 20 per cent. Land use is generally extensive, yields are low, and production per worker is far below other regions with similar resource endowments. This deficient productivity of the farm population is reflected in low incomes, which are generally below the equivalent of $100 per family per year. But from the developmental point of view, it is not so much the low level of present production but the slow rate of growth that counts most. Instead of spear-heading a dynamic development, agriculture has become a brake and, to some extent, the Achilles heel of the whole Latin economy. Development experts agree that to accomplish rapid and orderly urbanization and to stimulate industrial growth, agriculture must expand quickly and must supply the cities with larger and cheaper food supplies and raw materials. What is actually happening is that during the last decade total agricultural production in the region expanded at an average rate of a little less than 3 per cent, while domestic food production has grown only at approximately 2.5 per cent. This means that per capita growth of total agricultural output has remained far below other growth levels and that per capita food production has not improved at all. The shocking fact is that in the region as a whole, food production per person has fallen to a level lower today than it was before World War II.

There are, of course, significant regional variations with regard to countries and products. Yet, according to the latest report of the United Nations Economic Commission for Latin America, out of fourteen countries for which data are available (this includes all of the large ones), only six showed an increase in agricultural production exceeding population growth. In many countries a large part of the increases in production are attributable to export items, mainly tropical and semi-tropical products (such as bananas in Ecuador), which have had to contend with adverse world market trends. Thus, income received has lagged behind physical production. Perhaps the most unsatisfactory record is that of animal production (meat, milk, wool, eggs), growing at an annual aggregate of only 1.8 per cent. This situation can only accentuate the already precarious nutritional position of the large masses of Latin American families.

In the meantime, the continued migration to the cities and the growth in urban population have greatly increased the demand for marketed food. To fill the food gap, increasing amounts of Latin America's scarce foreign exchange earnings have had to be diverted from the purchase of capital goods to food imports. In 1960-61, these imports reached almost a half billion dollars, equivalent to the sum appropriated by the United States Congress as the initial investment in the Alliance for Progress. While there are obvious differences in growth rates among countries (with some countries, such as Mexico, experiencing relatively high rates of development), the over-all picture shows a largely stagnant agriculture, growing at rates below the minimum of 5 per cent a year laid down in the Punta del Este Charter, a net per capita decline in domestic food supplies, and an unsatisfactory growth of yields and technological progress.

Undoubtedly, there is no single or simple cause for this state of affairs, but Latin American intellectuals increasingly pinpoint the land system prevalent throughout the region as one of the main factors associated with this stagnation. The *latifundia-minifundia* pattern with its too large or too small production units, the system of indentured labor, the prevalent monopolies over land, water, and farm capital, the

general insecurity of titles, precarious tenancies, and the
general institutional environment of farming, all combine
to form a poor matrix for development. Raúl Prebisch,
longtime executive secretary of ECLA and an esteemed economist said recently:

> . . . The system of land tenure that still prevails in most Latin
> American countries is one of the most serious obstacles to eco-
> nomic development. . . . The land tenure system is charac-
> terized by extreme inequality in the distribution of land and
> of the income accruing from it. . . . Redistribution of the
> land pursues the following two basic objectives: to relieve social
> tensions by improving the distribution of property and income;
> and to increase productivity by creating conditions favorable
> to the introduction of modern techniques.[4]

The chief villain of this dismal state of affairs is the
latifundio, or the large estate. Much has been written about
the historical origins of the *latifundio* system. Historically,
it reflects the organization of society in Spain and Portugal
at the time of colonization and the superimposition of this
pattern on native cultures through large land grants. The
latifundio pattern has two main variants: the hacienda type
of extensively cultivated estates and the intensively worked
plantations. Each gives rise to quite different problems and
calls for different measures of reform.

The hacienda is typically a livestock-cereal operation with
a very low capital investment and little labor applied per
unit of land area. Ownership is often of the absentee type,
and labor is provided by the *colono* system or one of its
variants. The *colono* type of tenure is a tenant-worker arrangement operating in many Latin countries under various
names in which the farm family receives most, if not all, its

remuneration in kind, often as a temporary right to cultivate a plot of land in exchange for specified days of work and services to the landlord.

While there are notable exceptions, the hacienda system is inefficient both on the individual and national levels. Output per man and per land unit is low. The plantation, on the other hand, generally shows a high capitalization combined with stricter labor organization and controls. As a result, output per land unit is generally high, and farm efficiency is above average. Each system, however, embodies monopoly elements, and each results in extreme maldistribution of income and in conditions that destroy incentive for dynamic agricultural development.

The large holdings pre-empt most of the good land, squeezing the *minifundistas* (or occupiers of dwarf holdings) into the hills or onto poorer land. These *minifundia* have greatly multiplied during the last decades and have become even smaller through inheritance and subdivision. In Colombia, some 325,000 holdings average one-half hectare, and another half-million average two and one-half hectares. Three-fourths or more of all farms in Ecuador, El Salvador, Guatemala, Paraguay, the Dominican Republic, and Haiti are under five hectares. The vast majority of these *minifundia* represent a hand-to-mouth type of farming. Their possessors lack not only land but other productive resources such as credit and an effective access to markets. Their plots are frequently exhausted and eroding, and the peasants are at the mercy of unscrupulous tradesmen, truck owners, money lenders, lawyers, and petty officials. An undetermined but large number of these small farmers are squatters without a legal title to the parcels they occupy.

In a way, even the *minifundistas* may be better off than the mass of tenants, sharecroppers, and landless laborers who constitute the vast bulk of the agricultural population of most countries and provide the labor force (mostly seasonal) of the large farms. While official censuses notoriously underestimate these figures, in Chile half of the farm-labor force was classed as "landless workers." Corresponding figures for El Salvador are 53 per cent; for Ecuador, 42 per cent; and for Brazil, 38 per cent. If one adds the census categories of families who own no land to those who own less than five hectares, we get 91 per cent for Venezuela, 88 per cent for Honduras, 90 per cent for El Salvador, and 85 per cent for Panama and Guatemala.

The prevailing pattern of agriculture results not only in a wasteful use of land but, more importantly, in underutilization of human resources. Not only do the many millions of subsistence farmers make little or no contribution to the economy, but even the salaried farm workers are unemployed or underemployed during long periods. In few countries does the active farm-labor force work more than two hundred days a year, and in a number of places where mono-cultures predominate, the average is closer to one hundred days per year. Some of the most influential Latin American economists (generally of a "structuralist" orientation) see this tenure-linked farm-underemployment problem as the key factor underlying the low performance of agriculture, and also as the first line of the attack on general underdevelopment. For instance, Jacques Chonchol, a Chilean agricultural economist and prominent theoretician of the Christian Democratic party, has been arguing consistently for a massive program of capital formation via human investment plus labor-intensive farm development. He writes as follows:

> . . . From the economic point of view a radical agrarian re-
> form is a fundamental necessity to solve the problem of creat-
> ing productive occupation for the ever increasing rural pop-
> ulation . . . What is of basic importance is to find new pat-
> terns of social and political organization for Latin America,
> which, by using relatively small capital investments, would
> permit the productive use of this enormous reserve of human
> capacity, presently wasted . . . But I am convinced that this
> cannot be accomplished on the basis of the prevailing agrarian
> system which benefits a small privileged minority.[5]

In general, one can say that the typical Latin American
farmer is either a non-owning cultivator who has no stake in
the land he tills, no security, and little hope, or a *minifun-
dista* with a small plot of land and little else. He is likely
to be illiterate and often does not even speak the official
language of his country; he is in perpetual debt; and,
whether or not he works on the large estates, even if he per-
forms no personal service for the landlord, he feels the
pressures from above which keep him in his place. In short,
he is in a poor position to be launched on the road to progress.
A drastic change in his tenure status is needed to break the
many vicious circles of his plight.

To be sure, land tenure is not the only obstacle to farm
development, and there are other explanations for the poor
showing of agriculture. Prominent among these are the un-
favorable terms of trade, poor price policies, insufficient
capital, lack of education, lack of technical services, and
other similar problems. While all these are important, the
argument keeps returning to land ownership and to the roles
of the decision maker and worker on the farm. All the evi-

dence points to the crucial role of land tenure for the future of Latin American development. Some thoughtful observers, such as the late Sanford Mosk, have expressed the belief that at the bottom of Latin America's entire economic performance, so unimpressive when compared to the United States in historical perspective, is the colonial heritage of the land-tenure system.[6] But even taking a less sweeping view, there seems now to be considerable agreement that a much higher performance could be expected from Latin American agriculture—if land ownership were more diffused so that more farms were of "family-type" or medium size, if there were more owner-operator entrepreneurs, if clear land titles were generally the rule, if higher wages were paid to farm labor, if credit were not concentrated in the hands of a few, and if markets were accessible to all producers. These are, after all, the aims of most land reforms. Perhaps one should add here that not only would a reformed agrarian structure be more efficient but also that without reforms conventional developmental efforts are likely to be ineffectual. Further injections of capital, technical assistance, and other needed investments, even in much larger quantities, will be dissipated as long as the present land-tenure system prevails.

However, while there is some measure of agreement about these goals, there is much disagreement on the method, speed, magnitude, and priority of desirable action. What concerns us here is that Latin intellectuals, representative of a wide political spectrum, have opted for what William Glade has aptly called the "hacienda first" approach, that is, taking cultivated land from the large land-owners with minimal compensation, and re-distributing it among the cultivators.[7] One of the more articulate exponents of this point of view, Edmundo Flores, has written in his recent book

> . . . Land reform should not be confused with the introduction
> of efficiency in farming by means of hybrid seeds, extension
> services or the like. These measures, necessary as they are,
> do not basically alter income distribution or the social and
> political structure. Efforts to increase efficiency must be ap-
> plied *after* land reform takes place *not instead of it.* Producing
> more cotton, coffee, sugar, bananas or even maize, without
> changing the structure of land tenure, will not open new alter-
> natives for the *hacienda* or plantation workers and probably
> will not even raise their level of nutrition. . . . Land reform
> should not be confused with attempts either to reclaim un-
> productive land or to settle in uninhabited areas. . . . To be
> effective land reform has to *take productive land* (and its
> income) from the landlords without immediate compensation.
> . . .[8]

There are, of course, additional economic arguments in
favor of land reform which are based on broader considerations than the internal efficiency of the farming system itself.
Chief among these is the conviction that only an increase in
rural purchasing power can sufficiently enlarge domestic
markets for manufactured goods and associated services.
This realization of the interdependence between the rural and
urban sector of the economy and the crucial role of land
reform in widening the demand for all kinds of goods is
becoming one of the most powerful influences on economic
planning in the region. Victor Urquidi, an outstanding
Mexican economist, writes:

> The concentration of private property, especially agricultural,
> its inadequate use and non-use in economic activity, and the
> social and economic effects it produces constitute a funda-
> mental obstacle to Latin American Development. . . . Con-

centration results in large idle tracts of land, in stagnant farm technology, in the maintenance of the rural masses in a state of depressed demand, and in impediments to desirable demographic mobility. . . . the need for land reform today [i.e. to abolish the *latifundio*] is obvious. . . .[9]

In general, the intellectual pressure in favor of land reform as a strategic step to accelerate development on even narrowly economic grounds has become reinforced by the work of prominent Latin American economists and by the authoritative voice of practically all the international organizations working in Latin America, led by agencies of the United Nations, especially the FAO and the ECLA. The FAO, in particular, has been, since 1953, a vocal, vigorous, and persistent advocate of the strategic role of land-tenure reforms for Latin American agricultural development, often in the face of determined opposition by conservative groups.[10]

DISTRIBUTIVE JUSTICE

The second group of pressures militating for land reform belong in the socio-political sphere. They have to do with distribution of wealth, rights, opportunities, and power. Given the nature of land tenure as a determinant of the distribution of property income, these equity considerations may be even more important than those related more strictly to efficiency. Tenure-engendered inequalities, however, have a way of showing strong linkages to economic performance, so that defective tenure systems will prove to be inefficient because they are inequitable. Inequality of income should be considered first.

The concentration of landed property is the main cause

for the inequality of income distribution in Latin American agriculture. At the root of the trouble is the tenaciously prevalent hacienda system, a common heritage of the region, which, in one form or another, dominates the agrarian structure of all but a few of the Latin American countries. This system, in association with the plantation pattern of tropical areas, gives rise to the extreme concentration of land ownership found in Latin America, perhaps more severe than in any other comparable area of the world. The situation varies somewhat from country to country, but, on a whole, about 90 per cent of the farm land is held by less than 10 per cent of the farm owners. Normally, a very small minority of inter-locking family groups and commercial interests control an overwhelming percentage of the cultivated land. In Chile, 2.2 per cent of the farmers control three-fourths of the cultivated land. In Guatemala, 516 farmers control 41 per cent of the agricultural land. Half the farm land in Brazil is in the hands of 1.6 per cent of the owners.

A recently completed, exhaustive study by a team of United Nations experts in the five Central American countries shows the following figures: of the approximately 778,000 farms in these five countries, 621,000 (or almost 80 per cent) were smaller than the minimum deemed necessary to give a family sufficient employment and a minimum acceptable level of living. These farms together controlled some 12 per cent of the total amount of land in farms. On the other extreme, the largest 2,195 properties controlled 33 per cent of the farm acreage. If the next largest category is included, the statistics show 57,740 properties (7 per cent of the total) holding almost three-fourths of all farm land.[11]

In general, this pattern of land holding gives rise to income inequalities of tremendous proportions. Average incomes are already at a dangerously low level without even considering income distribution. ECLA estimates annual gross farm product per person at about $140 (1950 prices), while income per active worker is $400. Because of income disparities, it is probable that the great bulk of farm people have annual incomes below $100.

Some recent data from Costa Rica, a country not normally associated with extreme inequalities or social tensions, illustrate this point. In 1955, the average gross income per rural family equaled $1,200. This was about half of the average total family income throughout the economy. Within agriculture, 50,000 salaried workers had family incomes of only $584, and 16,400 small farmers averaged $591. Together they accounted for over two-thirds of the labor force in agriculture. One-fifth of the entire gross income was absorbed by 500 families, who averaged $42,000 each.[12]

Costa Rica, of course, is a Latin American country with a relatively favorable economic and social situation where the tenure system is not regarded as extremely inequitable. Data from the same United Nations project in a sample area of Guatemala, a country where 90 per cent of the farm population is included in the landless *minifundia* classes, indicate that the average income of these families is the equivalent of between $200 and $300—that is, income per person is between $40 and $60. Owners of large farms have family incomes of over $17,000. Many of these incomes are not earned, in the economic sense, but result from public investments diverted to the benefit of certain individual property owners, and from the overwhelming market and power position of the landlords. For instance, in typically inflationary situations, most agriculture credit is being converted into outright gifts. Since most institutional credit finds its way to the large landowners, they become the beneficiaries of such windfalls.

There is no question that the land-tenure system has been one of the main reasons for the emergence of dual societies in Latin America. The upper-bracket income recipients have increasingly patterned their way of life on the Western examples of upper-middle groups. This way of life has not only contributed to widening the already great social gap, but has also, in many cases, distorted the desirable structure of investments to favor the importation of consumer goods in the luxury class at the expense of capital goods and items for the mass market. A recent pertinent field study from Chile shows that in a representative sampling of large landowners with average disposable incomes of almost $50,000, 80 per cent of this income was spent on consumption, and most of it in categories that could clearly be classified as luxuries.[13] The most forceful recent statement on the crucial role of income redistribution for development and the need to curb the consumption of the rich was made by Prebisch, at Mar del Plata, in May, 1963:

> Should we preserve the existing system which through social inequality and privilege limits individual initiative? Or should we open it up widely by structural reforms in order to give it the full dynamic qualities it now lacks? . . . A re-distributive policy will insure that future increments of income will accrue to the inferior strata of the social pyramid . . . the superior strata (5% of the population), which accounts for three-tenths of the total consumption of Latin America, consume fifteen times more per family than the lower strata (50% of the population).

If this proportion could be reduced to eleven times, lowering consumption in order to raise investment, the annual rate of growth income per person could be increased from 1% to 3%. And if the proportion could be reduced to nine times, the rate of growth might rise to 4% or even more, according to the political possibilities of such an operation, and the aptitude of each country to carry it out. . . .[14]

And to leave little doubt about the sort of redistribution he is talking about, the author affirms a bit later:

. . . And thus one keeps hearing repeatedly from within and from the outside the old theme that we must first complete the stage of economic development and after that would come the social reforms; to talk of them now will stifle private initiative. *A profound error:* there will be no acceleration in the rate of economic development without a transformation of the social structure. . . .[15]

This, on a moment's reflection, is a most extraordinary statement with serious implications on developmental strategy. The relevance to drastic, rapid, and massive agrarian reforms is obvious, as Prebisch makes explicit in the second part of his paper.

There is some evidence that the income of the rural workers and *minifundistas* has actually decreased in the process of urbanization and that the gap between the "have's" and "have-nots" has become even wider. One of the few available income distribution studies with reference to Mexico indicates that not only have the various sectors of Mexican society shared unequally the benefits of the rather extraordinary contemporary development of that country, but that the lowest 20 per cent of the families have actually suffered a net decrease in their income. While the number of agricultural workers decreased by one-fourth in the last decade, they suffered a 10 per cent *per capita* net reduction in their earnings.[16]

The land-tenure status quo, as a distributor of wealth, income, and power, has come under increasing criticism on social grounds. The land-holding system, based on the hacienda, creates rigid social classes with little possibility of vertical or horizontal mobility. Worst of all, it perpetuates the false image of the peasant as an inferior being incapable of managing resources and of rising above his present situation. While the hacienda may have once fulfilled built-in social services, it no longer does. Nor does it permit the expansion and effective functioning of an education system, regarded by both friends and foes of land reform as an essential ingredient of developmental policy. The relationship between land tenure and educational opportunities are often subtle and not easily perceptible to conventional analysts who frequently maintain that without education the peasants are not ready for land reform. The fact that their unreadiness is closely related to their tenure status was clearly brought out by Solon Barraclough at a recent UNESCO symposium:

> The latifundia do not depend for their successful operation upon an educated work force supplemented by large numbers of extension agents, credit supervisors and home agents. In fact, such a development would destroy the system in short order. The traditional work relationships and social stratifications are based upon manipulating an uneducated, inarticulate and largely uninterested work force. The few special skills demanded such as herdsmen or even tractor drivers can easily be learned on the job without providing much general education first. Decisions come from above and workers are

99

not expected to think. A not uncommon experience for anyone who has worked much with plantations or other latifundia
is to hear the "administrador" vigorously damning the "uppity"
manners and disruptive independence of any worker who has
achieved and dares to show more than the average education
of his co-workers. . . . Even when socially-minded owners
build schools and provide similar services (as they occasionally
do) for their tenants, the "social vacuum" of the system nulli-
fies these efforts or so greatly dilutes them that the effects are
negligible. . . .

To understand why, one must also take into consideration the
worker's position in the system. Within the latifundia there is
almost no possibility of escape from his socially subservient
and economically dependent status. A very few may eventually rise to become foremen or mechanics but the road to advancement is generally blocked. The result is that the rural
family sees little value in sending their children to school at
all and no value at all in learning more than a bare minimum
of reading and arithmetic. This fact helps to explain the high
drop out rate in rural schools as well as the lack of drive to
build adequate facilities. . . .[17]

The traditional hacienda is crumbling, but its heritage
lives on. The prevailing pattern of land-holding and tenure
exerts a negative influence throughout the economic, social,
and political life of Latin America. It is either directly or
through its thousand invisible linkages indirectly associated
with a type of society in which privilege, gross inequality of
status and opportunity, and an inconceivable degree of
unfreedom prevail. Thus land reform comes to mean not so
much a technological solution or an attempt to adjust the
imbalance of resources but is identified, now more clearly
than ever, as a key part in the necessary reordering of human
relationships and social organization.

Explosive Forces

The foregoing paragraphs have discussed two main currents of intellectual argument for land reform which are increasingly penetrating public consciousness in Latin America. They represent pressures in the sense that economic policy makers, long accustomed to ignoring rural problems, are currently paying close attention to them. Until recently, the predominantly urban bias of Latin American statesmen combined with the determination of those in political power to maintain the status quo and to insure that rural-reform proposals would not affect national policies. But this position is changing rapidly. Latin American intellectuals, who are politically more articulate and influential than their counterparts in the United States, carry the land-reform banner. In such contexts these pressures are real enough. Yet, there now exist other, more concrete forces pushing for land reform, forces that are more likely to result in action, perhaps of a violent nature.

UNSETTLING DEVELOPMENT

Limited economic development itself is generating pressures which increase prevailing tensions. While the traditional hacienda functioned in a sort of closed circuit, there are now many unsettling influences, often of contradictory tendencies that are upsetting the old balance. For instance, rapid urbanization is creating labor shortages in some areas, while sporadic technical progress, especially mechanization, is producing localized unemployment. In some places the development of commercial agriculture is contributing to

101

the creation of a salaried labor force, better organized and more conscious of its situation than the old peons or *colonos*. For example, since 1959, Venezuela has had an important organized *campesino* movement which is actively pushing for a faster rate of land distribution. In Brazil and Chile, farm workers held their first national congress in 1961; the congress in Brazil was attended by 1,500 delegates and 3,000 observers from local peasant leagues and rural worker's unions.[18]

Better communications, the spread of radios and cinemas, and greater mobility for the people have brought the rural masses into more contact with the developed part of their countries and with the outside world. The demonstration effect of urban living and consumption patterns has become not only a stimulus toward new and better ways of life but also a powerful creator of dissatisfaction when the means for progress are blocked. Many of these unsettling influences, of course, are basically beneficial and essential for development. The point here is that where the means for change are not available, or where opportunities for progress in newly perceived directions are lacking, frustrations result. The tension among the urban proletariat in the swelling Latin American cities, which occasionally erupts in violence, is well known. But in the countryside such unsettling influences are rather new. Progress is being made, or rather some of the preconditions for progress are being created, but the danger is that the slow rate of change is likely to lead to the release of explosive rather than creative forces. In a relevant and thought-provoking paper, Roger Vekemans, a Jesuit sociologist, analyzes the possible disastrous consequences of these frustrations. He thinks that the frustrations created by limited development and the increasing "consciousness" of the masses, when confronted with the all too visible living-consumption patterns of the prosperous few and when up against the inaccessibility of resources on the one hand and the intransigence of the ruling groups on the other, are driven to "distributionist" and bitterly *revanchist* revolutionary activity. He deplores this probability as wasteful and as a diversion from the more desirable technological and self-directed, rather than class-oriented, revolution. He cites the "impermeable, impenetrable and arrogantly superior" attitude of the rich, who, instead of dedicating themselves to the job of fundamental development, are aping the affluent majorities of the developed Western World, as a perfect example of Toynbee's Herodian classes.[19]

Allan Holmberg, prime mover of the Vicos experiment, has this to say about the Peruvian case:

Both the caste structure of the society and the latifundia system of the Sierra are destined to disappear. In fact, they are already doomed. The question is whether they will disappear in a fairly gradual and orderly manner, as has happened in parts of the coast, or whether this change will take place suddenly and by more drastic means, as in Mexico and Bolivia.

It is likely that, if given opportunities to develop a more progressive and optimistic outlook on the world, the Indians will adjust fairly rapidly to modern conditions and will assume a productive and responsible place in Peruvian national life.

It is no less true, however, that unless the Indian populations are increasingly provided with opportunities and assistance in changing their way of life and improving their lot markedly, present conditions of unrest and dissatisfaction can lead to more and bloodier revolutions, or, at the least, to extreme and continuing conflicts in the process of their adjustment to modern life.[20]

103

Thus, while tensions, if allowed to resolve themselves, may bring development, it can be seen that the process of development often generates its own unsettling forces. Some observers even go so far as to suggest that because of the extreme concentration of income and the resulting dual social structure in Latin America, the process of development necessarily involves a social revolution. One such incisive analyst is K. H. Silvert, who feels that meaningful steps toward economic growth will be accompanied by painful readjustments in income distribution and power diffusion. He worries over the neglect of these delicate and complicated repercussions of development by social scientists:

> . . . The relationship between economic development and social revolution has been banished like sex and religion from the polite conversation of most "economic developers," Latin American and North American alike. . . . "We "foment" economic change, but refuse to permit ourselves to investigate what else it may be that we are "fomenting."[21]

There is a strong implication in Silvert's writings that the greatest challenge of Castro to the United States is not in the politico-military sphere, but in convincing authoritarian-prone Latin Americans and demonstrating that the truly democratic growth of nation-states is compatible with rapid economic development. It is clear, however, that if this alternative to totalitarian solutions is to get a fair and full test, the resulting policies will still call for profound and painful change in the established order.

POLITICAL TENSIONS

The second area of explosive tensions related to land

104

reforms is in the political sphere. While one of the chief justifications for drastic changes in land systems are political unity and a national conscience expressed in a measure of stability (as achieved in post-reform Mexico), the issue in the initial stages of the process is deeply divisive. In the traditional Latin American political upheaval or "revolution," nothing changed except the composition of the ruling groups.[22] Land reform may have been injected now and then as a political platform or campaign promise, but nothing essential happened. Cuba has changed all that. The prospect of a profound social revolution has intensified the power struggle, and land reform has become, almost overnight, a prized party issue across the political spectrum. Every party, every major candidate, nowadays, must have a land-reform platform. The appearance of the land-reform problems as an open party issue may, of course, be a hopeful sign pointing to possible compromise action; but with the present power structure, it may also give rise to dangerous perversions of the legitimate political competition. This appears to be the case in the Peruvian and Guatemalan military take-overs of 1962 and 1963, motivated to an important extent by a fear of the land-reform orientation of APRA and of presidential contender Arévalo in Guatemala.

It must be pointed out here that in the present political climate land reform is a handy issue for irresponsible demagoguery and is so abused by many politicians, especially of the more radical wings. Empty promises, the making of violent attacks on all moderate proposals without offering viable substitutes, or the virtual blind monopolizing of the reform issue by certain parties in such a way as to preclude negotiation and compromise action, are all extremely damaging and add to the explosive tensions by stirring up expectations without doing anything else. But such behavior is also dangerous because it is symptomatic of an oversimplified conception of land reform, which ignores the essential relationship between tenure reform and agricultural developmental programs which must follow it. Herein lies one of the paradoxical and misunderstood aspects of this complex subject: conventional developmental measures without structural reforms are doomed to fail, but the effect of pure land-tenure shifts may also be nullified or greatly delayed if not accompanied by a massive dose of all sorts of assistance, and vigorous organization, in behalf of the beneficiaries. The dimensions of this follow-up effort in terms of money and other resources, new institutions, the mobilization of talent, and, above all, publicly stimulated assistance for human development, are only most dimly perceived by even the most sophisticated political personages. Thus one is confronted with the task of effecting land reform capable of accomplishing a double miracle: it must somehow break down the present power system by making a frontal assault on the *latifundia* (undeterred by "technical obstructionists"), and, immediately afterwards, must shift into an entirely different gear to allow for full mobilization for a battle of production and resource development (undeterred by political obstructionists). The potentially most explosive situation created by blind demagoguery appears to be the one which would achieve neither reform nor development.

Albert Hirschman, in his study of the processes that led to the passage of the Colombian land-reform law of 1961, is more hopeful about the chances of the political process to produce meaningful instruments of reform, at least where social unrest, worry over far-left electoral successes, and extraordinary rural violence have prepared the ground, as in the case of Colombia and to some extent in Chile. He thinks that a combination of fear and opportunity moves the politician, who "sponsoring land reform . . . makes powerful enemies, to be sure, but he also makes numerous friends."[23]

There is also a greater effort to capture rural votes; more farmers are acquiring the franchise, and at balloting time the *campesinos* are not as susceptible to landlord pressures as before. The most vocal are, of course, the parties of the far left, but other, more progressive parties, such as the Christian Democrats in Chile and Venezuela, have made land reform a cornerstone of their platforms. Venezuela is an example where the political appeal of the land problem has lasted even after reform legislation has been passed and a large-scale program initiated. The various factions of the original *Acción Democrática* party vie with one another in claiming to represent the true interests of the farmers, and one of the issues in the recent split of the left wing from Betancourt's party has been dissatisfaction over progress in land distribution.

Another increasingly important phenomenon in some countries is the growing conflict of interest among the new industrialists, the urban commercial powers, and the traditional landed elite. Some observers doubt that this cleavage is really important and maintain that the joint interests of these classes in the increasingly polarized political struggles override any differences over landed property. Yet, the successful passage of the São Paulo agrarian transformation bill in 1961 demonstrated that the new middle and upper

107

classes in the city can have a strong influence on land policies. Hirschman also believes that in the Colombian case the weakening of the power position of the *latifundistas* gave the reformers important allies. "Industrialists and even the progressive farm owners and operators cannot always be counted on to stand up in public for their backward, semifeudal brethren. . . ."[24]

It is easy to overestimate the effect of all this activity, especially in countries where landed interest and associated oligarchies supported by the military are still firmly entrenched, but the net result of intensified legitimate political activity, in addition to a good deal of clandestine agitation, is likely to hasten the day of reform.[25] The real test of Hirschman's optimistic thesis of the possibility of "reform-mongering" without total revolution will be the manner in which the new land-reform laws in Colombia and Chile are actually carried out. The passage of previously unattainable legislation with "teeth in it" may be indeed an important achievement; but, as Hirschman points out, politicians, confident that nothing of importance is going to change, often vote in favor of socially advanced laws which turn out to be inoperative because of lack of enforcement or clever obstruction.[26]

EXTERNAL FORCES

Closely associated with these domestic pressures, but operating on a different level, are the external forces pushing for agrarian transformations. Clearly, the strongest foreign influences emanate from Havana and from Washington. It is impossible to separate Castro's centripetal impact on strictly agrarian matters from the general revolutionary matrix of his appeal; but in the early years of the Cuban upheaval, the land-reform objectives were the best publicized and made the most profound impression on Latin America. How much of this influence remains today, after some disenchantments with both the methods of the Cuban land reform and the results so far obtained, is hard to assess. Although intellectual circles may have lost some of their enthusiasm for Castro, in the popular mind he still appears to provide a powerful rallying point for rural discontent and an example for peasant aspirations. Undeniably, Cuba also continues to exert a strong pressure on the ruling groups to "do something" before it is too late.

In the United States, land reform has suddenly, but not surprisingly, become a cornerstone of American policy toward Latin America. After a long history of neglect and the pursuance of traditional policies that tended to reinforce the existing system, American attitudes are finally shifting toward a recognition of the land problem in Latin America. Evidently, Cuba and the shadow of the Cold War over the hemisphere have had a strong influence in producing such a shift. A series of most extraordinary public statements have been issued from Washington. On March 31, 1961, President Kennedy stated in his White House address in which he launched the Alliance for Progress: ". . . Economic growth without social progress lets the great majority of the people remain in poverty, while a privileged few reap the benefits of rising abundance. . . ." In his message to the Punta del Este Conference, he called for:

. . . Full recognition of the right of all the people to share fully in our progress. For there is no place in democratic life for institutions which benefit the few while denying the needs of the many, *even though the elimination of such institutions may require far reaching and difficult changes such as land reform* and tax reform and a vastly increased emphasis on education and health and housing. Without these changes our common effort cannot succeed. . . .[27]

Other men close to the intellectual focus of the New Frontier, such as Kenneth Galbraith, Lincoln Gordon, and Chester Bowles, stated this same point in various ways at numerous occasions. For instance, W. W. Rostow, one of the President's leading advisers, suggested:

The income above minimum levels of consumption, largely concentrated in the hands of those who own the land, must be shifted into the hands of those who will spend it on roads and railroads, schools and factories rather than on country houses and servants, personal ornaments and temples.[28]

These became the ideas that inspired the reform content of the Alliance for Progress. Under the new policy, material aid and support are to be given to programs that widen the opportunities for the rural masses. Projects related to land reform are to receive top priority. It has even been said that future increments of aid are contingent upon the enactment of land-reform legislation and its vigorous implementation. To lessen the accusations of "intervention in domestic affairs," an elaborate network of inter-American arrangements has been created, but the great burden of carrying out this bold new policy rests on the United States.

There is much skeptical and cynical commentary on this new orientation of United States foreign policy. Comments on the Alliance almost invariably emphasize confusion, accusing Washington of naïveté at best and of insincerity and opportunism at worst. Many find it hard to believe in American sincerity and determination to sponsor social revolutions. They point to strong domestic resistance in Congress, among United States business interests (especially those active in Latin America), and to the almost unbroken front of reactionary governments in the region which are all too eager to outpromise each other on future reforms in order to qualify for financial aid, or which claim that such aid is needed without waiting for reforms in order to save them from communism and collapse. In a series of lectures given in Puerto Rico in 1961, Arnold Toynbee, one of the recent skeptics, argued that the United States would fail dismally in its new venture in Latin America unless there arose a hitherto unprecedented change in the American public consciousness genuinely in favor of social justice and a willingness to accept the consequences of such policy.[29]

Since our concern here is mainly with conflict, out of this general dilemma of whether or not a prosperous and increasingly stability-minded country can become a social reformer abroad, one can extract three issues of potential violent controversy. First, there is an unwillingness (or incapacity) to face the gravity and dimension of the central land-reform problem as a redistributive force directed against the *latifundia*. While some of the intellectuals make the correct noises, and while many of the top echelon policy-makers and their analysts clearly understand the main issue, the broad cadres of diplomats, foreign-aid officials, negotiators, and technicians whose task is to implement the Alliance do not seem to be in tune with the new line. The report of a recent seminar for AID personnel begins: "Agrarian reform should consist in peaceful evolutionary processes directed toward the development of rural societies comprised primarily of owner-operators of family-sized farms and of tenants who have the opportunity to become farm owners."[30] In much American literature the central land-reform theme is "better land use," which, of course, misses the whole point altogether. What has to be understood and faced up to is that in genuine land reform someone must lose and even get hurt.

Sometimes even the top-level officials seem to be speaking in contradictory terms. Here are two quotes from speeches by Teodoro Moscoso, United States Co-ordinator of the Alliance:

> The people of the U. S. are not prepared to support a large-scale effort which they think will result in the perpetuation of social and economic systems that are structured so as to benefit the few to the detriment of the many. . . . We are insisting on reforms as a condition of our material support to Latin America. We would rather withhold our assistance than to participate in the maintenance of a status quo characterized by social injustice. . . .[31]

> Agrarian reform . . . [as a big chapter in the Charter of Alliance] gave rise very quickly to the misconception that all that was wanted or needed was the splitting up of the large landed estates which were owned by a few wealthy men who also played a decisive role in controlling the political destiny of their countries. But it is not this simple. . . . I prefer to speak rather in terms of modernizing agriculture. By that we do not necessarily mean taking land away, dividing it up and re-distributing it, but orderly re-organization, including possible changes in land tenure, supervised credit and extension service, and farm-to-market roads. . . . This is the

rational way in which the Alliance is tackling the problem of agriculture. It is the right way. . . .[32]

Which is the more representative voice, that of the insistent social reformer tilting with the status quo, or of the orderly modernizer tackling farm-to-market roads? Perhaps it is just semantics, but the problem can be seen in its most acute form in direct confrontation of American government personnel with the new generation of Latin Americans. Be it around the conference table, in university seminars, or in field projects, they seem to be talking a different language!

The second conflict concerns the fears of the United States business community with regard to drastic land reforms, and the growing suspicion that land reformers and their ilk are really Marxists of various shades of pink and red hastening the doom of private enterprise. Foremost in the minds of businessmen are two of the essential ingredients of land reforms: expropriation (at below "market" values), and the prominent role of government as an instrument of reform. Obviously, these worries are greatest where United States investments in agricultural enterprises are substantial. Here are a few excerpts from a report by a group of twenty-five businessmen, headed by J. Peter Grace, president of W. R. Grace and Company, which was issued by the United States Commerce Department in January, 1963:

> The COMAP survey team found the younger business leaders of Latin America anxious to help the Alliance for Progress succeed but puzzled by what they regarded as a tendency to "export socialistic ideas to Latin America," when it seemed clear to them that private enterprise held the key to sound national development. . . .

. . . The new Latin American voices of social unrest which
are being heard on every side, together with the call for
socialistic solutions of economic problems, both worry and
intimidate the foreign investor, as indeed they do his local
counterpart, the domestic Latin American private investor.
. . . [There exists] an area of uncertainty as to the significance
of the Alliance for Progress policies with regard to land reform. . . .[33]

This conflict becomes most acute in a situation which
occurred recently in Honduras, where the long-dominant
United Fruit Company did everything in its power to block
passage of the new land-reform law, which was officially
encouraged by the United States government. Similar conflicts, which are bound to recur and intensify, have arisen in
Guatemala and Peru. Wherever there are American-owned
plantations (and associated processing plants), it may be
wise to prepare for the inevitable day of reckoning before
some of the Cuban experience is repeated.

Perhaps the very heart of the land-reform controversy
lies in the issue of expropriation. How to value and pay
for land taken is not only the central economic and political
question of any reform program, but it also raises the most
delicate ethical considerations. Most Latin American land
reformers have long accepted the justice and inevitability
of minimal and deferred compensation, but it usually comes
as a severe shock to Americans steeped in the tradition of
due process of law and just compensation for property, even
when no direct United States investments are involved.

Fernández y Fernández, whom most of his Mexican colleagues regard as a rather conservative thinker on agrarian
matters (he advocates changing the *ejidos* to family farms

operating in a free land market), writes, for example: "In a greater or lesser degree all land reforms have to involve confiscation."[34] Jacques Chonchol, who, as many others, favors payment based on declared value for tax purposes, said recently: ". . . Either we pay for the land, or we make land reform."[35] To achieve a degree of fairness or justice in land redistribution is, of course, always difficult and subject to the prevailing socio-political power balance; but it is especially complicated in situations that are the result of long series of injustices and in which the "legitimacy" of the very origins of landed property are questionable.

Confiscation of land is regarded by American business interests as an attack on all property, and thereby as an undermining of the foundations of the capitalist system. In practice, compensation may never actually be received even though legally specified, or the value of the final payments may be much reduced by inflation. Yet neither Mexico and Bolivia (where nothing was paid) nor Japan and Egypt (where the value of compensation was minimal) have abandoned capitalism because land has been expropriated. In Latin America, it is most unlikely that outside Venezuela meaningful, large-scale land reforms will occur without some confiscation. United States policy, if unwilling to condone such practices, will at least have to face up to them as inevitable consequences of the land-reform orientation of the Alliance for Progress.[36]

A closely related third area of conflict between United States and Latin American thinking on land reform concerns the ideologically sensitive issue of the family farm. This is the cornerstone of American thinking about land tenure

115

and the main distinguishing feature between Western and communist-inspired agrarian reforms. Yet, as a number of careful social scientists have pointed out, in the majority of Latin American countries there is little or no tradition of family farming as is known in the United States or western Europe, and landlordism is so ingrained in the cultural heritage of the *latifundio* that even the smallest farm owner often sets himself up as a miniature *patrón* hiring some poor landless family further down the social scale to work his plot for him. There is also the crucial problem of how to transform the large estates so that their income would be better distributed and efficiency furthered. The classical extensive hacienda is not such a difficult case, but the reorganization of the plantation calls for a variety of solutions, many of which in the present stage of Latin American development will have to be various types of co-operatives or state tenancies. This is dictated not so much by considerations of economy or scale (as widely believed) but by the extreme scarcity of management and organizing capacity. It is not implied here that the Soviet or Chinese system of *kolkchoz* or commune would become the model—on the contrary, the basis of the new agrarian structure will undoubtedly be some sort of peasant owner-operatorship—but that many countries will elect or will be obliged to experiment with new forms of tenure toward which United States political and technical attitudes are extremely hostile. In general, it may prove to be a great mistake to attempt to implant or even to expect forms of rural social organization based on American ideals of unrestricted private rights in land.

Yet, without minimizing these problems or ignoring the gravity of the United States dilemma, American policy now

116

has important repercussions and, if consistent, it will meet increasingly with a favorable response. There is probably more genuine good will and more sophistication in Washington's current efforts than most commentators have acknowledged. Although these attitudes are not shared by many of the lower-echelon administrators and technicians or by the representatives of United States public opinion, the architects of the Alliance are beginning to realize the explosiveness of their subject and the potential influence they could have with a bold and imaginative program.

RURAL UNREST AND VIOLENCE

Finally, the most powerful active force of all is the intensified rural unrest and violence evident in Latin America. There are increasing symptoms that the hitherto passive rural masses are awakening. All the previously mentioned pressures, as they directly affect the peasants or filter down to their level, set into motion a series of processes. These start with an increased consciousness of the farmers' present situation, proceed through an awareness of the possibilities of change, and may lead to open militancy and violence, often the only available outlet. The penetration of political agitators into the rural countryside has accelerated rural uneasiness. Peasant strikes, occupation of farms, burning, and pillaging have become more frequent. The most extreme manifestation of such unrest is the emergence of the organized peasant leagues in northeastern Brazil under the leadership of Francisco Julião and some unusual peasant activity in the Peruvian highland, inspired locally by Hugo Blanco. There is, also, little doubt that the large-scale rural violence in Colombia has a partial explanation in the prevailing insecurity and in the lack of satisfactory land-tenure conditions in a country still very much under a colonial pattern of land holding. Incidents of occupation of haciendas in the Indian areas of the Andean countries are becoming more frequent.

It is significant to note here the extraordinary peasant unrest during recent months in Mexico, a country where fundamental land reforms have long been accomplished. Yet one reads of land invasions, hunger strikes, army crackdowns, and bloody riots in widely separated rural regions of Mexico. In the drought-stricken North, according to *Hispanic American Reports* in March, 1963, thousands of peasant squatters in desperation moved onto the huge cattle farms in Chihuahua and Durango. *Paracaidistas* ("squatters") also invaded private lands in the states of Zacatecas, San Luis Potosí, Sonora, and Guerrero. Meanwhile, *campesinos* killed one another in battles over land in Oaxaca, Puebla, and Chiapas. Yucatan's henequen growers protested violently over lack of credit. In the drought-plagued Laguna district, where almost one hundred thousand farmers are left without rights to land, demonstrations and agitation follow one another. A newly independent peasant league was formed in January claiming a membership of one million and demanding immediate land distribution to "all the have-nots in the Mexican countryside."[37] While the reasons for these events are complex, it is clear that the Mexican land reform has left many problems undone and that subsequent development, spectacular as it was, has turned the country further and further away from the original social-welfare orientation.

The focal point of rural violence in Peru is in the La Convención Valley on the eastern slopes of the Sierra. Led by strong rural syndicates, the farmers seized the land of the absentee owners and, well-armed, have created a virtual rebellious enclave, restrained (but not subdued) only by large contingents of army troops from Lima. Notable, also, is the fact that the *junta* hastened to promulgate a special decree for the La Convención area, the first of its kind in Peru, with provisions for acquisition and distribution of hacienda lands.[38]

In Brazil, the *ligas* are a special regional phenomenon, and do not yet have much leverage on national policies of reform. A careful observer, Frank Bonilla, thinks that the pressure of the leagues is a new and disturbing element in the Brazilian power spectrum, which, for some, is a strong argument in favor of decisive, immediate action, and for others, "only conclusive evidence of the greater evils to come if further agitation and socialist reforms are allowed." "Possibly," he writes, "Brazil may never get a true rural reform until the *ligas* or some equivalent organization gains the strength to make effective demands on the parties and the government."[39]

The most candidly fascinating analysis of the Brazilian "pre-revolutionary" scene was made about a year ago by Celso Furtado, superintendent of SUDENE and minister of development. Furtado contends that the main danger today of an extreme leftish type of revolution is in rural Brazil rather than in the urban proletariat, because, while the industrial class has mobility and can organize, the farmers are part of a rigid society with no flexibility. He writes:

> . . . The peasant class in Brazil is much more susceptible to revolutionary influences of the Marxist-Leninist kind than

the urban classes, although the latter, according to orthodox Marxism, should be the spearhead of the revolutionary movement. This is so because ours is an open society for the industrial worker, but not for the peasant. In effect, our political system permits the urban groups to organize in order to press their claims within the rules of the democratic game. The situation of the *campesinos* is totally different. Since they have no rights whatsover, they cannot have *legal* claims or bargaining power. If they organize, it is assumed that they do so with subversive ends in mind. We get to the necessary conclusion that Brazilian society in its important rural sector is very rigid. . . . We should not forget that more than half of the Brazilian population is directly tied to the land. To the extent that this sector maintains its present rigidity, all peasant movements for reform will rapidly adopt revolutionary techniques of the Marxist-Leninist type.[40]

Extra-legal peasant pressures will undoubtedly become stronger throughout the region and will be a potent force in the development of future governmental attitudes. The peasants in most countries still lack proper outlets for expression, but there is a great deal of new activity in rural areas toward farm unions, *campesino* leagues, and other types of rural worker organizations. As there are few well-established channels of orderly change in the countryside, these forces are likely to lead to explosive struggles and may even become the catalysts for far-right or far-left totalitarian take-overs.

Conclusion

It may be concluded from this rapid interpretation that the land-reform issue in Latin America is becoming more acute and the struggles around it more dangerously explosive. The forces which exert pressures for action are a combination of many factors. There is now a greatly increased awareness among intellectuals and policy makers of the strategic role of agrarian transformation in economic and social development. Serious attempts are being made to prepare legislation and to include land-reform projects in development programs. In most places, however, these efforts are still frustrated by the ruling powers in the countries, by middle-class indifference, and by the lack of appropriations, organization, and trained personnel. Land reform has also actively entered the political process, especially as a campaign issue and as a means for attracting new rural votes. Considerable clandestine agitation and propaganda accompany traditional types of political activity with land-to-tiller appeal as their main theme. Limited economic development is adding to the other pressures by intensifying local imbalance, by widening the gap between the urban-commercial sectors and the rural masses, and by exaggerating the demonstration effect.

While many of these pressures, however painful, are important and necessary catalysts for development, concrete progress is very slow, and there is an alarming discrepancy between expectations and performance. This sense of frustration is manifest in sporadic, but greatly intensified, rural violence. If there were vigorous and visible movements toward the substitution of outmoded tenure systems, the sense of progress might outweigh other shortcomings.

The new attitude of the United States is a healthy departure from long acquiescence in, and support for, the status quo, but its net effect thus far has been small. Some thoughtful observers feel that meaningful large-scale changes in the land system will not come unless the whole political and

121

social matrix undergoes reform. In places where the historical process has led to extreme inflexibility and bitterness, genuine land reform may also be incompatible with a predominantly capitalistic organization of economic life and certainly with a continuation of traditional United States business activity. If the gradualist theory of reform without undue structural shock fails, the Alliance for Progress and United States Latin American policy will undergo severe strains. With the land question occupying a central role in expected revolutionary changes, the probability of unpalatable political situations, short-run food deficits, and other unpleasant circumstances is increasing. It is also likely that reform solutions will, in many places, drastically depart from American-sponsored models based on family farming. All these prospects call for an unusual measure of patience and enlightenment from all levels of United States policy-making. Understanding of the explosive forces in land reform and the development of a sympathetic and helpful attitude toward emerging new situations, which on close reflection may be less objectionable than that which now exists, are among the more fascinating challenges facing this hemisphere.

1. *Que São as Ligas Camponesas?* ("Cadernos do Povo Brasileiro," Vol. I [Rio de Janeiro, 1962]), pp. 75-76.

2. For recent information on Latin American land-reform development, see Inter-American Development Bank, *Social Progress Trust Fund—First Annual Report* (Washington, D. C., 1961) and *Second Annual Report* (Washington, D. C., 1962). See also Thomas F. Carroll, "The Land Reform Issue in Latin America," in *Latin American Issues—Essays and Comments*, ed. Albert O. Hirschman (New York, 1961), pp. 161-201.

3. "Conditions for Economic Change in Under-Developed Countries," *Journal of Farm Economics*, XXXXIII, No. 4 (November, 1951), p. 695.

4. "Economic Aspects of the Alliance," in *The Alliance for Progress—Problems and Perspectives*, ed. John C. Dreier (Baltimore, 1962), pp. 38-41.

5. *La Reforma agraria en America Latina* (Conferencia Pronuncia da en la Escuela de Estudios Económicos Latino-Americanos para Graduados de la Universidad de Chile, en Junio de 1962), pp. 13-15.

6. Sanford A. Mosk, "Latin America versus the United States," *American Economic Review*, XLI (May, 1951), 367-83.

7. William Glade, "Social Backwardness, Social Reform and Productivity in Latin America," *Inter-American Economic Affairs*, XV, No. 3 (Winter, 1961), 3-32.

8. *Land Reform and the Alliance for Progress* (Princeton, N.J., 1963), pp. 8-9.

9. *Viabilidad económica de América Latina* (México, 1962), pp. 86-87.

10. For example, the FAO has organized two regional seminars of wide impact on land problems (Campinas, Brazil, in 1953, and Montevideo, Uruguay, in 1959), both of which, but especially the first, were influential in arousing interest in the subject, encouraging open debate on such controversial matters, and demonstrating that land-reform issues were amenable to social-science analysis.

11. Sergio Maturana, *Las relaciones entre la tenencia de la tierra y la eficiencia del uso de recursos agrícolas en Centro América* (Proyecto Tenencia de la Tierra y Condiciones de Trabajo Agrícola en Centro América), (San José, Costa Rica, 1962).

12. *Tenencia de la tierra en Centro América* (Document presented by FAO to a UNESCO seminar on Social Research and Problems of Rural Life in Central America, Mexico, and the Caribbean Region), (Mexico City, October, 1962), UN/UNESCO/SS/SRRL/C-4.

13. Marvin J. Sternberg, "Chilean Land Tenure and Land Reform" (Ph.D. Dissertation, University of California, Berkeley, 1962).

14. "Hacia una dinámica del desarrollo Latinoamericano," in Comisión Económica para América Latina, *Suplemento de comercio exterior* (México, April, 1963), pp. 5-6.

15. *Ibid.*, p. 9.

16. Ifigenia M. de Navarrete, *La distribución del ingreso y el desarrollo económico de Méjico* (México, 1962).

17. *Agrarian Structure and Education in Latin America* (Paper prepared for a conference on Education and Social and Economic Development in Latin America, Santiago, Chile, March, 1962), UNESCO/ED/CEDES/30, pp. 16-17.

18. United Nations, "Social Development in Latin America" (Chap. xi), *Report on the World Social Situation*, E/CN.5/375/Add.2, March 4, 1963, p. 25.

19. Roger Vekemans, "Análisis psico-social de la situación pre-revolucionaria de América Latina," *Mensaje* (Santiago, Chile), No. 115 (December, 1962), pp. 647-55.

20. Allan R. Holmberg, "Changing Community Attitudes and Values in Peru: A Case Study in Guided Change," in *Social Change in Latin America Today* (New York, 1960), p. 74.

21. *The Island and the Continent* (Latin American Development and the Challenge of Cuba), American Universities Field Staff, Reports Service, "East Coast South American Series," VIII, No. 1 (January 29, 1961), p. 8.

22. This point is analyzed by Merle Kling in "Towards a Theory of Power

and Political Instability in Latin America," *Western Political Quarterly*, IX, No. 1 (March, 1956), 11-35. Kling wrote of these "palace revolutions": "A leader may be assassinated or exiled, a new junta may assume the posts of political authority, but control of the economic bases of power is not shifted and the hierarchy of social classes is not affected; in short, there is no restructuring of society" (p. 25).

23. Albert O. Hirschman, *Journeys toward Progress—Studies of Economic Policy Making in Latin America* (New York, 1963), p. 156.

24. *Ibid.*, pp. 155-56.

25. Lowry Nelson, who in his *Rural Cuba* has accurately diagnosed the pre-Castro rural social scene, feels that large-scale farm uprisings may neither be possible nor necessary for reform. He writes in a private comment: "We have sent hundreds of millions of dollars worth of weapons to Latin American nations, but it is doubtful if the peasants got any of it. What I am saying is, I suppose, that revolutions a la Cuba, Bolivia, Mexico are quite unlikely to happen. My other point—and the main one—is that changes are taking place in the power structure involving a shift to the urban-industrial sector. And while the hacendados have their colleagues there among the bankers, industrialists, etc., the *votes* are not among them but rather among the workers. These workers are in large part, ex-peasants and are allies of the peasants in the struggle for social justice. I suspect that the only 'green risings' in the future will be not national, but local, here and there. And they will be ruthlessly suppressed by the boys with the machine guns. I think the ballot now has more possibility and will have in the future, than bullets. Let's get the peasants organized and educated! And don't send the poor devils up against the guns. Perhaps some kind of 'civil disobedience' can be developed; a few sit-ins adapted to the hacienda."

26. Hirschman, *op. cit.*, pp. 156-57.

27. Message from President Kennedy, "Alliance for Progress, a Program for the Peoples of the Americas," *Department of State Bulletin*, XLV, No. 1157 (August 28, 1961), 355-56. (Italics added.)

28. *The Stages of Economic Growth: A Non-Communist Manifesto* (Cambridge, 1960), p. 19.

29. *The Economy of the Western Hemisphere* (New York, 1962).

30. *Latin American USOMs Seminar on Agrarian Reform* (Washington, D. C.: International Co-operation Administration, 1961), p. 1.

31. "Social Change and the Alliance," in *The Alliance for Progress—Problems and Perspectives*, ed. John C. Dreier (Baltimore, 1962), pp. 94-95.

32. "Address by the Honorable Teodoro Moscoso before the Wisconsin Union, University of Wisconsin, Madison, Wisconsin, March 28, 1963," press release, Agency for International Development, Friday, March 29, 1963.

33. *Proposals to Improve the Flow of U. S. Private Investment to Latin America: Report of the Commerce Committee for the Alliance for Progress, a Group of 25 Businessmen, Chaired by J. Peter Grace, President of W. R. Grace & Co.* (Washington, D. C., January 4, 1963).

34. Ramon Fernández y Fernández, *Economía agricola y reforma agraria* (México, 1962), p. 146.

35. Chonchol, *op. cit.*, p. 26.

36. For a refreshingly frank but gloomy view on the role of confiscatory practices in developing countries, see M. Bronfenbrenner, "The Appeal of

Confiscation in Economic Development," *Economic Development and Cultural Change*, III, No. 3 (April, 1955), 201-18.

37. *Hispanic American Reports*, XVI, No. 1 (March, 1963), 14-19.

38. Decreto-Ley No. 14444 (Aplicación de la reforma agraria a los Valles de la Convención y Lares), (Lima, March 28, 1963).

39. "Rural Reform in Brazil," *Dissent*, IX, No. 4 (Autumn, 1962), 378-79.

40. "Reflexiones sobre la pre-revolución Brasileña," *El Trimestre Económico*, XXIX (3), No. 115 (July-September, 1962), 381. A revised English version of this paper was published in *Foreign Affairs*, XLI, No. 3 (April, 1963), 526-35.

NUTRITION AND THE
POPULATION EXPLOSION
IN
LATIN AMERICA

ARNOLD E. SCHAEFER

TODAY'S accelerating growth in world population stirs the imagination of a few, creates severe pessimism in some, strikes the passive ears of others, and receives cheers from still others. (To support the latter view, one has only to note the industrial or Wall Street forecasts of increased sales for every production from diapers to homes.) Since 1945, death rates in the developing countries have dropped suddenly as a result of newly discovered "miracle" drugs, medicines, insecticides, and massive public health programs such as malaria eradication. But this drop in death rate has caused severe population pressures: first, because the land space of the earth is fixed, and second, because population is growing in geometrical proportion.

Seen in historical perspective, increases have not been rapid until recent years. At the time of Christ, the population of the world is estimated at 250 million. By 1600, this number had doubled to 500 million with starvation, disease, and the ravages of war holding average population growth rates to well under 1 per cent a year. By 1940, however, the average annual increase in world population reached 1 per cent; a little over two decades later, in 1961, it was 2 per cent. At this latter rate, the world's present population of three billion will increase to twenty-three billion in one century. With a 3 per cent increase, it will reach 60.3 billion in the same period.[1] Population increases (Table 1) are

TABLE 1

COMPARISON OF BIRTH AND DEATH RATES,
PERCENTAGE OF INCREASE IN POPULATION,
AND POPULATION IN SELECTED AREAS
OF THE WORLD

	Annual Birth Rate per 1,000	Annual Death Rate per 1,000	Percentage of Annual Rate of Increase	1959 Population (In Millions)
Latin America.....	41	16	2.5	201
Africa................	45	26	1.9	236
Europe...............	19	11	0.8	423

highest in the underdeveloped areas of Latin America (2.5 per cent); Asia (2.3 per cent), excluding Japan; and Africa (1.9 per cent). These figures can be compared to Europe (0.8 per cent) and Canada and the United States (1.7 per cent).

It should be noted that in Latin America the percentage of annual population increase varies from country to country and from area to area. For example, the temperate region of southern South America shows an annual rate of increase of 1.4 per cent for Argentina and 1.3 per cent for Uruguay as compared to 3.5 per cent for Central America (Table 2).

TABLE 2

RATES OF ANNUAL POPULATION INCREASE IN CERTAIN
COUNTRIES IN LATIN AMERICA*
(latest available figures)

Country	Birth Rate per 1,000	Death Rate per 1,000	Percentage of Annual Rate of Natural Increase
Dominican Republic, 1953-58 (estimated)			3.5
Costa Rica, 1959	42.0	9.0	3.4
Mexico, 1960	45.5	11.4	3.4
Nicaragua, 1953-58 (estimated)			3.4
El Salvador, 1960	44.8	10.8	3.4
Guatemala, 1960	50.0	17.9	3.2
Brazil, 1961			3.1
Venezuela, 1953-58 (estimated)			3.0
Chile, 1959	35.4	12.5	2.3
Argentina, 1960	22.3	8.1	1.4
Uruguay, 1953-58 (estimated)			1.3

*For Costa Rica, Mexico, El Salvador, Guatemala, Chile, and Argentina, see *United Nations Demographic Yearbook, 1960*. For Brazil, see Population Reference Bureau, "Population Profile," April 2, 1962. For the others, see Department of Statistics, *Pan American Union Release 4117a6*, No. 700, July 27, 1960.

A decline in population-growth rates in Latin America cannot be expected in the near future. In Europe and America the transition from high to low rates of population growth was very slow, extending over a period of about 150 years. Now with death rates dropping and birth rates remaining constant or rising, it appears that populations in the developing areas will grow so large as to defy efforts to

129

improve economic and social conditions necessary to bring about a decline in the rates of population growth. Eugene Black, former president of the World Bank, has stated, for example: "Population growth threatens to nullify all our efforts to raise living standards in many of the poorer countries."[2]

Population pressures undoubtedly increase unrest in developing countries. Per capita income in these countries as a whole is approximately $100 per year, as compared to $850 in Western Europe and $2,350 in the United States. If populations in Latin America and other areas continue to rise, these figures will not change appreciably. In fact, many believe the gap will widen. Marriner S. Eccles, former chairman of the Federal Reserve Board, has said: " . . . nothing is more important than to understand the economic, social, and political dangers of the world's failure to control its population growth. Democracy cannot survive, much less expand, unless the standard of living of the backward countries of the world is substantially improved. This is an impossible task unless the population growth is curbed."[3] The expectations among the peoples of the developing countries for a rapid rise in living levels are creating powerful pressures which have and will tend to lead to violent internal revolutions.

The developing countries being plagued with population explosions have many common denominators:

1. A very high proportion of the labor force engaged in agriculture, and heavy pressure of population on land currently under cultivation

2. Widespread malnutrition

3. A high incidence of disease; poor health, especially maternal

and child health; inadequate medical services; few hospitals; few doctors; lack of sanitation; and lack of a pure
water supply

4. No adequate food-processing industry, food standards, controls, and specifications

5. Poor roads, communications, and transport

6. Inadequate supply of power and light

7. High illiteracy and low educational level

8. A low per capita income and rate of savings and investment

9. Low industrial output in relation to population

Taken together, these hindrances to economic and social
progress become entwined in a vicious cycle. High birth
rates create overcrowding and promote disease, thereby undermining health and reducing productivity; low productivity, in turn, means low income and reduced savings.

Nutrition has played a significant role in the population
explosion in the developing areas. In a recent book, Dr.
Jacques M. May has described the nutritional state of man.
May sees man as governed by separate yet interrelated basic
geographical patterns, four in number:

1. Medical geography—diets and nutritional diseases

2. Human geography—man's traditions and culture

3. Economic geography—food production and resources

4. Physical geography—land and water environment, tempera-
ture, latitude, and rainfall

These patterns, states May, must all be taken into account in
an attempt to improve the nutritional state of the developing
nations, to make them prosperous, stable, and peace-loving.[4]
Too often, however, not all of these factors are taken into
account, and attempts are made to impose other attitudes

131

or morés on people with entirely different backgrounds and values.

Recently the United States has begun to sponsor health and nutrition programs in Latin America and other areas of the world, but for the most part, she has spent a very small percentage of her total foreign aid on such programs. In 1960, the total expenditure for health and nutrition (including United States aid to United Nations agencies) was $84,000,000, less than 3 per cent of the foreign-aid budget of approximately $3,000,000,000. The sum expended by the government on nutrition as such, represented by the Interdepartmental Committee on Nutrition for National Defense (ICNND), was equal to less than 0.5 per cent of the $84,000,000 (Table 3).

Table 3

APPROXIMATE CONTRIBUTIONS BY THE UNITED STATES GOVERNMENT
TO INTERNATIONAL HEALTH ACTIVITIES—FISCAL YEAR 1960*

Mutual Security Program

Malaria eradication	$32,000,000	
All other international co-operation administration programs	20,639,000	
Project HOPE	2,336,000	
United Nations Children's Fund	12,000,000	
United Nations Expanded Technical Assistance	2,198,000	
Other	2,811,000	
Total		$71,984,000
Assessed payments of World Health Organization, Pan American Health Organization, and International Educational Exchange		7,000,000
Medical research grants overseas by national institutes of health		5,133,000
Total		$84,117,000

*See draft report of the Nutrition Advisory Group Meeting of the Pan American Sanitary Bureau, Washington, D. C., January, 1962.

132

Despite limited funds, ICNND has played a leading role in nutrition and health programs in Latin America. In January, 1962, upon recommendation of the Organization of American States, the Pan American Health Organization convened a nutrition advisory group to develop suitable health programs for Latin America. The OAS statement declared that improvement in health conditions was absolutely essential for economic growth. The OAS clearly recognized, however, that such measures would create new population pressures. The statement flatly declared that the younger age groups not only would increase faster than their countries could develop economically, but they also would live longer than their forebears. For the OAS, however, the answer to this dilemma was to improve the nutritional state of Latin Americans and to carry out economic and social reforms. At the Punta del Este meeting, Resolution Number 2 of the Alliance for Progress stated, in part: " . . . to make substantial improvement in the feeding and nutrition of the most vulnerable sectors of the community by increasing the consumption of animal or vegetable protein; to reduce the rate of mortality in children under five years of age to one half of its present rate during the present decade. . . ." This committed the United States and participating governments of Latin America to health and nutrition measures which would increase the population but would improve its well-being at the same time. Nutritional plans were necessarily to become a part of an over-all national health plan. This, in turn, was to be incorporated into broader economic and social development measures.

Land resources have become a vital matter in solving nutritional problems. In Latin America there are approximately five million additional mouths to feed each year.[5] This additional five million demands one and one-half million metric tons of wheat simply to meet its caloric needs. The fact that only 7 per cent of the arable land is now under cultivation, however, gives rise to the hope that this requirement can be met by putting new lands to productive use. At present, only 29 per cent of all land in Latin America is estimated to be wasteland.[6] Even now, the soil of Latin America provides the world with most of its sugar and coffee, which, in a sense, are luxury and not nutritious foods. At the same time, many inhabitants still use agricultural systems and techniques dating from pre-Columbian times and live on the few indigenous staples they raise on small holdings, reducing the productive capacity of the land.

Unbalanced land distribution constitutes another facet of the same problem. According to a report of a group of experts from the Organization of American States, between 3 and 8 per cent of the landowners in Latin America own 60 to 80 per cent of the cultivatable land; inversely, 75 to 80 per cent of all land holdings account for only 5 to 10 per cent of the total cultivated acreage. Low purchasing power is likewise a deterrent in Latin America. A skilled worker in many countries must work three and one-half to four and one-half hours to earn enough to purchase a kilogram of meat or thirty to fifty minutes to buy a liter of milk.[7]

The poor state of education in Latin America also inhibits nutritional progress. The educational level for the area as a whole is two years of schooling. Forty per cent of the population over fifteen years of age is illiterate, and at present the number of illiterates is estimated at forty million. Over fifteen million children of school age have no educational facilities whatsoever, and less than 10 per cent of the children who enter the first grade complete their primary education.

Public health and sanitation are serious problems. Owing to the extremely poor sanitary conditions under which the vast majority of the people of Latin America live, the incidence of infectious diseases is high. Because of the deteriorating state of nutrition, the duration and severity of these diseases becomes greater and greater. The mortality figures for Latin America indicate that in the age group of one to four years there are, in some areas, 300 deaths due to malnutrition for every one which occurs in more highly developed countries.[8] Since it has been shown that in many countries most deaths of children suffering from malnutrition are reported and tabulated as due to gastrointestinal or respiratory infections, this figure does not reflect the real magnitude of the loss of lives or manpower due to malnutrition. Moreover, malnourished children are more susceptible to other infectious diseases. Investigations on the actual cause of death have demonstrated that in some areas of Latin America up to 40 per cent of the children in the one-to-four age group die with signs of acute protein caloric malnutrition, and many more die in the course of relatively brief episodes of either diarrhea or some other infectious disease.

To deal with these problems the United States has sponsored nutrition programs in Latin America through the Interdepartmental Committee on Nutrition for National Defense (ICNND). Supported by the State, Defense, Agriculture, Health-Education-and-Welfare departments, the Agency for International Development (AID), and the Atomic Energy Commission (AEC), ICNND carries on an international multidisciplinary program aimed at improving the nutritional status of peoples in developing countries.[9] It is the only co-ordinated broad nutritional program in the world. Since 1956, ICNND has assisted twenty-three developing countries that had previously ignored the basic needs of the vast majority of their populations for proper and adequate food and health. Its program has been a co-operative, scientific, and training endeavor using a people-to-people and scientist-to-scientist approach.

Advising the committee is a panel of consultants who are specialists in the fields of medicine, biochemistry, nutrition, agriculture, food technology, and economics. Teams of scientists and specialists, 350 in all, obtained from thirty-five colleges and universities and from governmental agencies, have gone into all corners of the world to work side by side with approximately one thousand of their scientific counterparts. To date, collaborative studies in Latin America have been conducted in Peru, Ecuador, Colombia, Chile, Uruguay, and Bolivia. In 1963, teams are scheduled to make surveys in Brazil and Venezuela. In the surveys already conducted the committee has worked very closely with the Pan American Health Organization, the United Nations Children's Fund (UNICEF), the Food and Agriculture Organization of the United Nations (FAO), and the World Health Organization (WHO).

Where ICNND teams have operated in South American areas, they have made valuable comparisons of food consumption patterns.[10] Corn is the principal cereal produced in the tropical countries of South America, although considerable quantities of rice are grown in the lowlands. On the other hand, significant amounts of wheat are imported (Table 4). Cassava earns the dubious distinction of being virtually the least nourishing of any staple food. Not only is cassava deficient in protein but the biological value of its protein is very low. One hundred grams of the edible portion of cassava root, for example, supply only 150 calories and 0.8 grams of protein compared with 360 calories and ten grams of protein for the same weight of wheat. Other protein-calorie ratios of cereals and tubers are given in Table 4.

TABLE 4

PROTEIN-CALORIE RATION OF LOW-PROTEIN FOODS (EDIBLE PORTION)*

	Grams of Protein Per 1,000 Calories
Wheat	29
Corn	24
Rice	19
Potatoes	24
Plantain	17
Cassava	5

*Interdepartmental Committee on Nutrition for National Defense, *INCAP-ICNND Food Composition Table for Use in Latin America* (Bethesda, Md.: National Institutes of Health, 1959).

Comparison of food patterns between tropical and temperate countries indicates that the possibility of protein malnutrition is much greater in tropical countries (Table 6). With respect to animal products and total calories, the pattern of food consumption in temperate areas is comparable to the norm for Western Europe. In Argentina and Uruguay, for example, the availability and consumption of meat are similar to those patterns for the United States and Europe (Tables 5 and 6).

Besides identifying major nutrition problems, one of the primary objectives of ICNND surveys is to define ways and means by which a given country or specific area within that

TABLE 5

CONSUMPTION OF CEREALS IN SOUTH AMERICAN COUNTRIES, 1960*
(kilograms per person per year)

	Wheat	Corn	Rice	Other Cereals	Per Cent of Calories Obtained from Grain
Tropical countries					
Colombia	13.8†	46.7	13.9	0.9	33.7
Venezuela	33.6†	35.3	7.3	7.3	35.5
Ecuador	13.5†	30.1	13.8	18.5‡	38.0
Peru	33.2†	25.1	19.9	9.1	42.2
Bolivia	19.9†	42.7	9.1	16.6‡	51.3
Brazil	26.8†	30.0	37.5	0.5	33.0
Paraguay	31.0†	29.8	6.6	......	28.5
Temperate countries					
Chile	112.5	5.1	7.1	6.0	50.0
Argentina	111.6	5.9	4.9	8.7	39.0
Uruguay	92.2	3.3	8.1	3.0	36.0

*D. B. Hand, A. E. Schaefer, and C. S. Wilson, "A Comparative Study of Food Consumption Patterns in Latin America, Middle Eastern and Far Eastern Countries," in First International Congress of Food Science and Technology, *Proceedings* (London, September, 1962).

†Largely imported.
‡Mostly barley.

country can better utilize its own resources. For example, a team may suggest locally produced supplemental foods, which could readily substitute for milk or animal products and alleviate protein malnutrition problems. Approximately fifty foods produced and consumed throughout Latin America in the categories of legumes, seeds, and nuts can supply from ten to forty-four grams of protein per one hundred grams of edible product and may be used in place of milk or meat.[11]

In order to make practical recommendations such as these, it is essential to ascertain in detail nutritional problems and their implications, especially food consumption patterns of

138

TABLE 6

ESTIMATED CONSUMPTION OF SELECTED PROTEIN-POOR AND PROTEIN-RICH
FOODS IN SOUTH AMERICAN COUNTRIES, 1960*

(kilograms per person per year)

COUNTRY	PROTEIN-POOR FOODS				PROTEIN-RICH FOODS		
	Sugar	Potatoes†	Cassava	Bananas	Pulses	Meat	Fish
Tropical countries							
Colombia	44	32	44	107	6	32	2
Venezuela	31	30	28	157	14	23	1
Ecuador	28	68	6	142	11	18	5
Peru	27	98	25	69	10	22	5
Bolivia	26	57	17	30	6	29	1
Brazil	41	30	154	63	22	35	3
Paraguay	23	33	179	10	11	71	1
Temperate countries							
Chile	29	88	......	2	10	30	20
Argentina	37	69	5	13	2	117	4
Uruguay	31	48	......	5	1	108	2

*D. B. Hand, A. E. Schaefer, and C. S. Wilson, "A Comparative Study of
Food Consumption Patterns in Latin America, Middle Eastern and Far Eastern
Countries," First International Congress of Food Science and Technology,
Proceedings (London, September, 1962).

†White potatoes and sweet potatoes.

principal population groups. (An example of the type of
data collected by the ICNND nutrition teams is given for Chile
and Ecuador in Table 7.) In addition to dietary information,
teams evaluate medical problems by clinical examinations
and biochemical assessments. Estimates are also made of the
potential for agricultural improvement and development of
a particular food industry, while teams grade and define
major nutritional problems (Table 8).

So far nutrition surveys carried on in Chile, Peru,
Ecuador, Colombia, and Bolivia indicate that the problems
of feeding the growing population of Latin America are

TABLE 7

Representative Diet Patterns*

	Chile	Ecuador (Lowlands)	Ecuador (Highlands)
Type of diet	wheat	rice	corn
Number of families	278	116	213
Number of people	1,640	757	1,322
	Grams Consumed per Person per Day		
Cereal and cereal products			
Bread	311	35.5	39.4
Wheat products	40	......	......
Rice	23	122.1	78.8
Corn	......	2.3	116.2
Other	5	25.3	34.3
Sugar	50	45.4	58.5
Meats			
Beef and mutton	81	66.1	41.6
Pork	9	......	......
Poultry	10	......	......
Fish and shellfish	33	21.8	......
Milk and milk products	107	124.1	267.7
Eggs	8	7.8	1.9
Fats and oils	27	37.9	11.1
Vegetables			
Leafy, green and yellow	97	57.6	38.1
Potatoes and other tubers	153	125.6	275.2
Tomatoes	16	29.6	6.2
Other	46	19.9	20.8
Pulses	27	20.4	39.0
Fruits			
Citrus fruits	5	21.1	13.1
Bananas	6	99.3	19.2
Other	96	0.3	......
Miscellaneous	19	14.7	14.3

*United States Interdepartmental Committee on Nutrition for National Defense, *Chile—Nutrition Survey* and *Ecuador—Nutrition Survey* (Bethesda, Md.: National Institutes of Health, 1960 and 1961).

TABLE 8

Prevalence of Nutrition Problems in Seven Countries as Revealed by ICNND Surveys*

Country	Ariboflavinosis	Avitaminosis A	Thiamine Deficiency	Vitamin C Deficiency	Goiter	Anemia	Protein Deficiency	Caloric Deficit
Military Personnel								
Peru.........................			B	C		B		
Civilian and Military Populations								
Ecuador................	B	C		B	B	B	B	B
Chile.....................		C		C		B	B	B
Colombia..............	C		C	C	A	B	C	C
West Indies...........	A	B	C	C	A	A	C	
Uruguay...............					B			
Bolivia..................	A	B		B	B	B	B	B

KEY

A: General nutrition problem.

B: Problem in a special area of the country or among special groups.

C: Problem manifested by clinical, biochemical, or dietary evidence in special areas or groups.

*See the following surveys: United States Interdepartmental Committee on Nutrition for National Defense, *Peru—Nutrition Survey of the Armed Forces* (1959); *Ecuador—Nutrition Survey* (1960); *Chile—Nutrition Survey* (1961); *Colombia—Nutrition Survey* (1961); *Uruguay—Nutrition Survey* (1960); *Bolivia*—Initial Report of the Nutrition Survey of Bolivia (1962), (Bethesda, Md.: National Institutes of Health).

numerous and diverse. In Chile, for example, the Foreign Agricultural Service of the United States Department of Agriculture has tabulated a food-balance table, representing the estimated total amount of food available for consumption, assuming there is an equitable distribution among all members of the population. This table shows that in 1960, Chileans should have consumed 2,700 calories per person per day. Actual dietary intake studies made by the ICNND revealed, however, that the average caloric consumption was 2,200 calories and that many factors operated to keep this figure low.[12] Transportation for Chile's food products and refrigeration facilities are grossly inadequate. Chile lacks marketing and food processing facilities for maximum food preservation, a fact which leads to short life for food and high wastage. Sanitation is also poor. All of these factors result in a loss of about 25 per cent of Chile's food. On the other side, the quality of food grown in Chile is excellent, and progressive programs are under way to improve the indicated defects. It is estimated that Chile has a potential agricultural capacity to feed four to five times her present population.

Although the nutrition survey in Peru was concentrated primarily on military personnel, assessment of agriculture production and food availability suggested several large problems which limit the quality and variety of food available for the population.[13] There is need to improve a system of collection of statistics concerning production so that the adequacy of the national food supply may be more accurately determined. It is necessary to develop improved transportation and better storage and marketing procedures to insure a more equitable distribution of foods. Agricultural production also suffers from a shortage of land available for that purpose. Only 2 per cent of the country's total land area is under cultivation or used for pasture. Since 1940, the population has increased 40 per cent, but less than 20 per cent more land has been brought under cultivation during this period. Thus, food production has not kept pace with population growth and more imported food has been required, although the Peruvian government has instituted irrigation projects designed to provide a substantial increase in the arable land. Steps are also being taken to improve yields per hectare. Further benefits may ensue from the governmental decree which stipulates that more farm land in the coastal area that is now used for cotton and sugar must be devoted to food crops. In addition, Peru has an unlimited, relatively untapped resource in its fishing industry, which has so far been directed primarily toward export of fish meal to the United States and not toward local consumption.

Ecuador can produce almost any agricultural food product by proper soil management, fertilization, and insect control.[14] The coastal region has become one of the world's leading producers of bananas, cocoa, coffee, and rice, which through export account for practically all of Ecuador's foreign exchange. Examples of some progress made in agriculture in Ecuador are: (1) Milk production has been raised in some herds from an average of six pounds of milk per day in 1955 to nearly twenty pounds in 1958; and (2) Fertilized plots at San Alfonso yielded 7,350 pounds of potatoes per hectare as compared to 2,294 pounds from unfertilized plots. A major deterrent to such increases in other crops, however, is the fact that nearly all fertilizers are imported.

Credit is one factor inhibiting progress. In Ecuador credit

for development in agriculture and food processing is difficult to obtain. An Ecuadorian farmer or food processor, for
example, may request a loan from a bank. The bank, in turn,
calls in a private investor who agrees to provide the money
at 12 per cent interest for three or four months. Similar
loans for rice farmers for the growing season only (three to
four months) cost 20 per cent of the over-all basic loan which
is charged as interest.

Cost of land is also a problem. In spite of the steep slopes
and hills, arable land in the sierras of Ecuador costs about
$400 to $800 per acre. This is in sharp contrast to the land
prices (generally at $30 or less per acre) in the coastal
regions.

The problems of food production, processing, and distribution in Colombia are many, but the advances being made
in both facilities and application of technical knowledge are
impressive.[15] During the period 1948-58, the production
of barley, rice, potatoes, and wheat has made significant
gains, and the prospects of further increases are very bright
indeed. A new hybrid variety of corn now developed in
Colombia has a potential of increasing yields by 20 to 40
per cent. Also, a new wheat breeding program has resulted
in the development of two new varieties which not only
increase the yield by 30 to 40 per cent but, even more important, reduce the time interval for maturity from 185 days
to 145 days, thus permitting a yearly two-crop rotation.

From a nutritional standpoint, one discouraging statistic
in Colombia is that the production of dry beans and pulses
during the past ten years has remained stationary with a
price increase of nearly threefold, from thirteen cents to
thirty-four cents per pound. An ordinary, inexpensive, good

144

plant protein thus costs the consumer nearly as much as beef protein. In addition, much of the bean acreage in the Cauca Valley has been displaced by cotton. Research efforts to solve this problem are now being directed toward the development of acceptable, cheap, nutritionally adequate plant protein mixtures for the supplementary feeding of infants and school children, utilizing such raw materials as cottonseed, peanut, fish, and bean meals.

In Bolivia prospects are not so bright.[16] The daily available per capita supply of 1,880 calories is the lowest of any of the South American countries, despite the fact that over two thirds of the Bolivian population obtain their living from agriculture. Estimates based on the 1950 census indicate that 30 per cent of the total land area of Bolivia is classified as farm land, but only 2 per cent is under cultivation, and only 10 per cent of this relatively small area is irrigated.

In summary, the population explosion in Latin America is not a prediction but a reality. Since 1945, widespread adoption of health measures has brought a sudden drop in death rates, especially in infant mortality. In no other major area of the world is population growing at a faster rate. Resulting population pressures are both a cause and an effect of nutrition and health programs instituted in Latin America. It is perhaps one of the great paradoxes of this age that steps taken to improve the well-being of the people of the developing nations have created the very population pressures that make economic and social progress so difficult.

In the realm of nutrition, however, prospects are not altogether bleak despite population pressure. In some areas, such as Colombia, use of new agricultural techniques has greatly increased the yields of certain foods. In Chile it is estimated that the land can produce food for four to five times her present population if proper marketing and food processing facilities are developed. With only 7 per cent of the potential arable land of Latin America under cultivation, there is also hope that many new areas will be put to use, producing crops that will improve the nutritional state of Latin America. The United States, through its universities, experiment stations, and ICNND, has two of the major ingredients necessary to assist Latin America in improving the nutritional well-being of its developing nations. First, the United States has the technical know-how for food production, processing, and distribution (food industry). Second, various private and governmental agencies have the technical and research information in the field of health and nutrition. The latter contribution has been instrumental in creating population pressures, but in some areas gains made in the food-industry field have more than outstripped population-growth rates. In other areas, like Bolivia, however, there are still a great many problems to be resolved.

Some observers believe that the rate of population growth will slow with economic and social development; but in order to make real progress in this direction, the developing countries must move forward in many fields simultaneously—in education, health, agricultural production, research, extension work, training for its indigenous personnel, public finance, and development of food industries. In the face of population pressures, such progress will demand both sacrifice and outside assistance, but economic development may yet occur and bring, concomitantly, the hoped-for decline in population growth.

146

1. Center for International Economic Growth, *Does Overpopulation Mean Poverty?* (Washington, D. C., 1962), p. 14.

2. *Ibid.*, p. 23.

3. *Ibid.*, p. 21.

4. Jacques M. May, *The Ecology of Malnutrition in the Far and Near East* (New York, 1961), p. 3.

5. Draft report of the Nutrition Advisory Group Meeting of the Pan American Sanitary Bureau (Washington, D. C., 1962).

6. *Ibid.*

7. *Ibid.*

8. *Ibid.*

9. A. E. Schaefer and F. B. Berry, "United States Interests in World Nutrition," *Public Health Reports 75*, No. 8 (1960), pp. 677-86.

10. See D. B. Hand, A. E. Schaefer, and C. S. Wilson, "A Comparative Study of Food Consumption Patterns in Latin America, Middle Eastern and Far Eastern Countries," in First International Congress of Food Science and Technology, *Proceedings* (London, September, 1962).

11. United States Interdepartmental Committee on Nutrition for National Defense, *INCAP-ICNND Food Composition Table for Use in Latin America* (Bethesda, Md.: National Institutes of Health, 1961).

12. United States Interdepartmental Committee on Nutrition for National Defense, *Chile—Nutrition Survey* (Bethesda, Md.: National Institutes of Health, 1961).

13. United States Interdepartmental Committee on Nutrition for National Defense, *Peru—Nutrition Survey of the Armed Forces* (Bethesda, Md.: National Institutes of Health, 1959).

14. United States Interdepartmental Committee on Nutrition for National Defense, *Ecuador—Nutrition Survey* (Bethesda, Md.: National Institutes of Health, 1960).

15. United States Interdepartmental Committee on Nutrition for National Defense, *Colombia—Nutrition Survey* (Bethesda, Md.: National Institutes of Health, 1961).

16. United States Interdepartmental Committee on Nutrition for National Defense, *Bolivia—Initial Report of the Nutrition Survey of Bolivia* (Bethesda, Md.: National Institutes of Health, 1962).

THE CULTURE
OF
POVERTY*

OSCAR LEWIS

ALTHOUGH a great deal has
been written about poverty and the poor, the concept of a
culture of poverty is new. In this essay, I shall present a
conceptual model of the culture of poverty in terms of a con-
figuration of a large number of interrelated traits of which
poverty is a crucial one, and I shall illustrate a few of these
traits with some of my favorite passages from *The Children
of Sánchez.*

To those who believe that the poor have no culture, the
concept of a culture of poverty may seem like a contradiction
of terms. It would also seem to give to poverty a certain
dignity and status. This is not the intention here. In anthro-
pological usage the term *culture* implies, essentially, a design

*In this essay, the author draws extensively from his work *The Children
of Sánchez: Autobiography of a Mexican Family* (New York: Random House,
1961) with the generous permission of the publisher.

for living which is passed down from generation to generation. In applying the concept of culture to the understanding of poverty, I want to draw attention to the fact that poverty in modern nations is not only a state of economic deprivation, of disorganization, or of the absence of something; it is also something positive in the sense that it has a structure, a rationale, and defense mechanisms without which the poor could hardly carry on. In short, it is a way of life, remarkably stable and persistent, passed down from generation to generation along family lines. The culture of poverty has its own modalities and distinctive social and psychological consequences for its members. It is a dynamic factor which affects participation in the larger national culture and becomes a subculture of its own.

The culture of poverty, as here defined, does not include primitive peoples whose backwardness is the result of their isolation and underdeveloped technology and whose society, for the most part, is not class stratified. Such peoples have a relatively integrated, satisfying, and self-sufficient culture. Nor is the culture of poverty synonymous with the working class, the proletariat, or the peasantry, all three of which vary a good deal in economic status throughout the world. In the United States, for example, the working class lives like an elite compared to the lower class of the less developed countries. The culture of poverty would apply only to those people who are at the very bottom of the socio-economic scale, the poorest workers, the poorest peasants, plantation laborers, and that large heterogenous mass of small artisans and tradesmen usually referred to as the lumpen proletariat.[1] In the United States Lloyd Warner's concept of the "lower-lower" comes closest to the culture of poverty.

It is important to distinguish between impoverishment and the culture of poverty. Not all people who are poor necessarily live in or develop a culture of poverty. For example, middle-class people who become impoverished do not automatically become members of the culture of poverty, even though they may have to live in the slums for a time. Similarly, the Jews who lived in poverty in eastern Europe did not develop a culture of poverty because their tradition of literacy and their religion gave them a sense of identification with Jews all over the world, a sense of belonging to a community united by a common heritage and common religious beliefs.

The culture or subculture of poverty comes into being in a variety of historical contexts. Most commonly it develops when a stratified social and economic system is breaking down or is being replaced by another, as in the case of the transition from feudalism to capitalism or during the industrial revolution. Sometimes it results from imperial conquest in which the conquered are maintained in a servile status which may continue for many generations. It can also occur in the process of detribalization such as that now going on in Africa, where tribal migrants to the cities are developing "courtyard cultures" remarkably similar to the Mexico City *vecindades*. Many observers are prone to view such slum conditions as transitional or temporary phases of drastic culture change. But this is not necessarily the case, for the culture of poverty is often a persisting condition even in stable social systems. Certainly in Mexico it has been a more or less permanent phenomenon since the Spanish conquest of 1519 when the process of detribalization and the movement of peasants to the cities began. Only the size, location, and composition of the slums have been in flux. Similar processes have undoubtedly been going on in many other countries of the world.

The culture of poverty has some universal characteristics which transcend regional, rural-urban, and even national differences. In my book *Five Families* (New York: Basic Books, 1959), I suggested that there were remarkable similarities in family structure, interpersonal relations, time orientations, value systems, spending patterns, and the sense of community in lower-class settlements in London, Glasgow, Paris, Harlem, and Mexico City.[2]

In Mexico, the culture of poverty includes at least the lower third of the rural and urban population. This population is characterized by a relatively higher death rate, a lower life expectancy, a higher proportion of individuals in the younger age groups, and, because of child labor and working women, a higher proportion of gainfully employed. Some of these indices are higher in the poor *colonias* or sections of Mexico City than in rural Mexico as a whole.

The culture of poverty in Mexico is a provincial and locally oriented culture. Its members are only partially integrated into national institutions and are marginal people even when they live in the heart of a great city. In Mexico City, for example, most of the poor have a low level of education and literacy, do not belong to labor unions, are not members of a political party, do not participate in the medical care, maternity, and old-age benefits of the national welfare agency known as *Seguro Social,* and make very little use of the city's banks, hospitals, department stores, museums, art galleries, and airports.

The economic traits which are most characteristic of the

culture of poverty include the constant struggle for survival, unemployment and under-employment, low wages, a miscellany of unskilled occupations, child labor, the absence of savings, a chronic shortage of cash, the absence of food reserves in the home, the pattern of frequent buying of small quantities of food many times a day as the need arises, the pawning of personal goods, borrowing from local money lenders at usurious rates of interest, spontaneous informal credit devices (*tandas*), and the use of second-hand clothing and furniture.

Some of the social and psychological characteristics include living in crowded quarters, a lack of privacy, gregariousness, a high incidence of alcoholism, frequent resort to violence in the settlement of quarrels, frequent use of physical violence in the training of children, wife beating, early initiation into sex, free unions or consensual marriages, a relatively high incidence of the abandonment of mothers and children, a trend toward mother-centered families and a much greater knowledge of maternal relatives, the predominance of the nuclear family, a strong predisposition to authoritarianism, and a great emphasis upon family solidarity—an ideal only rarely achieved. Other traits include a strong present-time orientation with relatively little ability to defer gratification and plan for the future, a sense of resignation and fatalism based upon the realities of their difficult life situation, a belief in male superiority which reaches its crystalization in *machismo* or the cult of masculinity, a corresponding martyr complex among women, and finally, a high tolerance for psychological pathology of all sorts.[3]

Many of the traits of the culture of poverty can be viewed as attempts at local solutions for problems not met by existing institutions and agencies because the people are not eligible for them, cannot afford them, or are suspicious of them. For example, unable to obtain credit from banks, they are thrown upon their own resources and organize informal credit devices without interest. Unable to afford doctors, who are used only in dire emergencies, and suspicious of hospitals "where one goes only to die," they rely upon herbs or other home remedies and upon local curers and midwives. Critical of priests "who are human and therefore sinners like all of us," they rarely go to confession or mass and rely upon prayer to the images of saints in their own homes and upon pilgrimages to popular shrines.

A critical attitude toward some of the values and institutions of the dominant classes, hatred of the police, mistrust of government and those in high position, and a cynicism which extends even to the church gives the culture of poverty a counter quality and a potential for being used in political movements aimed against the existing social order. Finally, the culture of poverty also has a residual quality in the sense that its members are attempting to utilize and integrate into a workable way of life the remnants of beliefs and customs of diverse origins.[4]

The people in the culture of poverty have a strong feeling of marginality, of helplessness, of dependency, of not belonging. They are like aliens in their own country, convinced that the existing institutions do not serve their interests and needs. Along with this feeling of powerlessness is a widespread feeling of inferiority, of personal unworthiness. This is even true of the slum dwellers of Mexico City, who do not constitute a distinct ethnic or racial group and do not suffer from racial discrimination. In the United States the culture

154

THE CULTURE OF POVERTY

of poverty of the Negroes has the additional disadvantage of racial discrimination.

People with a culture of poverty have very little sense of history. They are a marginal people who know only their own troubles, their own local conditions, their own neighborhood, their own way of life. Usually, they do not have the knowledge, the vision, or the ideology to see the similarities between their problems and those of their counterparts elsewhere in the world. They are not class conscious, although they are very sensitive indeed to status distinctions. When the poor become class conscious, members of trade-union organizations, or when they adopt an internationalist outlook on the world, they are by definition no longer part of the culture of poverty, although they may still be desperately poor.

The concept of a cross-cultural subculture of poverty enables Americans to see that many of the problems thought of as distinctively American or distinctively Negro problems (or those of any other special racial or ethnic group) also exist in countries where there are no distinctive ethnic groups involved. It also suggests that the elimination of physical poverty per se may not be enough to eliminate the culture of poverty which is a whole way of life. One can speak readily about wiping out poverty; but to wipe out a culture or sub-culture is quite a different matter, for it raises the basic question of respect for cultural differences.

Middle-class people, and this would certainly include most social scientists, tend to concentrate on the negative aspects of the culture of poverty. They tend to associate negative valences to such traits as present-time orientation and concrete versus abstract orientation. I do not intend to idealize or romanticize the culture of poverty. As someone has said, "It is easier to praise poverty than to live in it"; yet some of the positive aspects which may flow from these traits must not be overlooked. Living in the present may develop a capacity for spontaniety, for the enjoyment of the sensual, the indulgence of impulse, which is often blunted in the middle-class, future-oriented man. Perhaps it is this reality of the moment which the middle-class existentialist writers are so desperately trying to recapture but which the culture of poverty experiences as natural, everyday phenomena. The frequent use of violence certainly provides a ready outlet for hostility so that people in the culture of poverty suffer less from repression than does the middle class.

In this connection, one might take exception to the trend in some sociological studies to identify the lower class almost exclusively with vice, crime, and juvenile delinquency, as if most poor people were thieves, beggars, ruffians, murderers, or prostitutes. Certainly in my own experience in Mexico, I found most of the poor to be decent, upright, courageous, and lovable human beings. As the novelist Henry Fielding perceptively noted, "The sufferings of the poor are indeed less observed than their misdeeds."

Some of this ambivalence in the evaluation of the poor is reflected in literature. On the positive side are many proverbs glorifying the state of the poor as something greatly to be respected. Well-known instances can be cited, as from the gospel of Saint Luke:

Blessed be ye poor: for yours is the kingdom of God.

From Henry Thoreau's *Walden:*

It is life near the bone, where it is sweetest.

156

From Edward Moore's *Hymn to Poverty:*

> Poverty! Thou source of human art,
> Thou great inspirer of the poet's song!

From Thomas Gray's *On the Pleasure:*

> Happier he, the peasant far,
> From the pangs of passion free,
> That breathes the keen yet wholesome air
> of ragged penury.

From Shakespeare's *All's Well That Ends Well:*

> My friends are poor but honest.

Or from Menander's *The Lady of Leucas:*

> The poor are the protégés of the Gods.

On the other hand there are many negative stereotypes about poverty, such as from the Babylonian *Talmud* chronicles:

> All the days of the poor are evil.

Miguel de Cervantes in *Don Quixote* writes:

> He must have a great deal of godliness who can find any satisfaction in being poor.

From *Ecclestiasticus* comes:

> The life of the poor is the curse of the heart.

And from Arnold Bennett-Maugham,

> If you've really been poor, you remain poor at heart all your life.

Finally, Bulwer-Lytton writes:

> Poverty makes some humble, but more malignant.

—a view in the vein of the English proverb,

> The devil wipes his tail with the poor man's pride.

And many today seem to agree with Hartley Coleridge when he asked,

> What can a poor man do but love and pray?

In short, some see the poor as virtuous, upright, serene, independent, honest, secure, kind, simple, and happy, while others see them as evil, mean, violent, sordid, and criminal.

Many people in the United States find it difficult to think of poverty as a stable, persistent, ever-present phenomenon, because the American expanding economy and the especially favorable circumstances of American history have led to an optimism which makes Americans believe that poverty is transitory. As a matter of fact, the culture of poverty in the United States is indeed of relatively limited scope, although it is probably more widespread than has been generally recognized.

In considering what can be done about the culture of poverty, one must make a sharp distinction between those countries in which it represents a relatively small segment of the population and those in which it constitutes a very large section. Obviously, the solutions will have to differ in these two areas. In the United States, the major solution proposed by planners, social-work agencies, and social workers in dealing with what are called "multiple problem families," the "undeserving poor," or the so-called hard core of poverty has been to attempt slowly to raise their level of living and incorporate them into the middle class. And, wherever possible, there has been some reliance upon psychiatric treatment in an effort to imbue these "shiftless, lazy, unambitious people" with the higher middle-class aspirations.

In the undeveloped countries, however, where great masses of people live in the culture of poverty, a social-work solution does not seem feasible. Because of the magnitude of the problem, psychiatrists can hardly begin to cope with it. They have all they can do with their growing middle class. In the United States, delinquency, vice, and violence represent the major threats to the middle class from the culture of poverty. In the United States there is no threat of revolution. In the less developed countries of the world, however, the people who live in a culture of poverty may one day organize into a political movement which seeks fundamental revolutionary changes. This is one reason their existence poses terribly urgent problems.

If one were to grant what has briefly been outlined here as the basic psychological aspect of the culture of poverty, then it may be more important to offer the poor of the world's countries a genuine revolutionary ideology rather than the promise of material goods or of a quick rise in the standard of living. It is conceivable that some countries can, without materially increasing the standards of living, eliminate the culture of poverty (at least in the early stages of their industrial revolution) by changing the value systems and attitudes of the people so they no longer feel marginal—so they begin to feel that it is their country, their institutions, their government, and their leadership.

A few of the many traits of the culture of poverty can be illustrated by some excerpts from *The Children of Sánchez*. The Sánchez family consists of Jesús Sánchez, the father, and his four children by his first wife. Jesús, age fifty, has had four wives, never less than two at a time. His children are Manuel, thirty-two, Roberto, twenty-nine, Consuelo, twenty-seven, and Marta, twenty-five.

Manuel, the eldest son, was born in Mexico City and has lived all his life in crowded one-room slum apartments. He left primary school in the sixth grade, married in free union at age fifteen, and was a widower with four children at age twenty-eight. He has worked throughout his childhood at a great variety of jobs. He was a vendor of lottery tickets, newspapers, and singing birds, a shoemaker, a baker, a glass and leather worker, and a temporary agricultural laborer in the United States. His life story illustrates the fact that although the lives of the poor may be difficult, they are by no means dull. He says: "Mexicans, and I think everyone in the world, admire the person 'with balls,' as we say. The character who throws punches and kicks, without stopping to think, is the one who comes out on top. The one who has guts enough to stand up against an older, stronger guy, is more respected. If someone shouts, you've got to shout louder. If any so-and-so comes up to me and says, 'Damn your mother.' I answer, 'Damn your mother a thousand times.' And if he takes one step forward and I take one step back I lose prestige. But if I go forward, too, and pile on and make a fool out of him, then the others will treat me with respect. In a fight, I would never give up or say, 'Enough,' even though the other was killing me. I would try to go to my death smiling. That is what we mean by being *macho*, by being manly.

"Life around here is raw, it is more real, than among people with money. Here, a boy of ten is not scared off at the sight of the female sexual organ. Nor is he shocked when

160

he sees a guy lifting someone's wallet, or using a knife on a man. Just having seen so much evil at close range makes him face reality. After awhile, even death itself doesn't frighten us. We get our bruises in the struggle against life at a very early age, see? And a scab begins to form. It never disappears, like a blood scab, but remains permanently on our spirit. Then, there comes another blow and another scab, until it gets to be like a kind of armor which makes us indifferent to everything."[5]

While Manuel was married in free union to his first wife, Paula, with whom he had four children, he also carried on a love affair with Graciela, neglecting his wife and children. After Paula's death he hoped to settle down with Graciela permanently, but at this point she left him and went off with another man. Having lost both women in his life, he remained despondent until his friend and *compadre*, Alberto, suggested that they leave for the United States as agricultural workers *(braceros)*. Manuel agreed and went to California with his *compadre*, Alberto; but Alberto, while working in the fields, took sick and underwent a gall-bladder operation in a hospital. Manuel felt he should be with his *compadre* so he feigned illness, complaining that he had a bellyache. At the hospital, they examined him, prescribed an ice pack, and sent him back to work. Manuel played sick again, and this time he lost his appendix. As Manuel put it, "I lost my appendix because I didn't speak English and they didn't speak Spanish."[6] "I spent seventeen days in that hospital. The insurance company took care of everything . . . a very pretty room, luxurious beds with radios in the headboard . . . telephone in the room . . . everything that was out of our reach in Mexico. It didn't cost us a single penny.

"I really felt like somebody in California! Everybody treated me well, both in the hospital and on the job. I liked the life there, even though I found its form too abstract, too mechanical, in the sense that the people were like precision machines. They have a day, an hour, a fixed schedule set up for everything. It must be a good method because they have lots of comforts. But the government charges them a tax for food, for shoes, for absolutely everything. If our government tried that tax business here, I believe it might even cause a revolution. A person doesn't like to have what's his taken from him.

"The *braceros* [the temporary agricultural workers] I knew, all agreed on one thing, that the United States was '*a toda madre*.' That means, It's the best. Every once in a while someone complained . . . like Alberto, who said that the Texans were lousy sons-of-bitches because they treated Mexicans like dogs. And we looked badly upon the discrimination against the Negroes. We had always thought of American justice as being very strict and fair . . . we didn't think that money or influence counted there like it did here. But when they put a Negro on the electric chair for rape, and let a white go for the same thing, well, we began to realize that American justice was elastic, too.

"But we all noticed that even the workers who were not so well off, had their car and refrigerator. When it came to equality and standard of living, well, they'd lynch me for saying this, but I believe that the United States is practically communistic . . . within capitalism, that is. At least it was in California, because I even heard a worker shout at his boss, and the boss just shut up. The workers there are protected in lots of ways."[7]

Manuel then goes on, however, to indicate that within the culture of poverty, envy and cynicism are powerful drives.

"Even if you live on the bottom level, you have to feel higher up. I've seen it among the trash pickers; there's rank even among thieves. They start arguing, 'You so-and-so, all you steal is old shoes. But me, when I rob, I rob good stuff.'⁸

"The thing is, there is no equality here. Everything is disproportionate. The rich are very rich, and the poor are infamously poor. There are women with babies in their arms and a few more hanging onto their skirts, going from door to door to beg for food. There are plenty like my Uncle Ignacio, who gives their women three pesos a day for expenses [that is 24¢ a day], and others who don't know where the next meal is coming from, with nobody to give a thought to them. If the rich people knew how the poor managed to exist, it would seem like a miracle to them.

"Look, when a rich man throws an orgy, some of those *fiestas* or receptions those millionaires in Lomas make, in one night they spend enough to support a whole orphan asylum for a month. If they would come down off their pedestals to share the lives and see the misery of their countrymen, I believe out of their own pockets they would install electricity, sewage, and do something to help. If I were rich, I would ease the pain of the poor, at least some of those closest to me, and let them have a few necessities. But who knows? Maybe if I were a rich guy sailing in my boat or traveling in an airplane, I wouldn't remember anymore, eh? The poor stick to the poor . . . they know their place . . . and the rich, well, they go to the Hilton. The day I dare go to the Hilton, I'll know there has been another revolution!

163

"I don't know about political things . . . the first time I voted was in the last election . . . but I don't think there is much hope there. We can't have any kind of social welfare for the working people, because it would be used only to make the leaders rich. The men in the government always end up rich and the poor are just as badly off. I have never belonged to a union, but my friends who do say they can be fired at any time without indemnification, because the union leaders and the bosses make agreements among themselves. Yes, we have a long way to go down here. I tell you, progress is a difficult thing."[9]

Now Manuel sounds more upward mobile and sophisticated than he really is. Actually, he firmly believes in destiny, an attitude very typical in the culture of poverty. When he was in his early twenties, he tried to go into business repairing shoes, which failed for various reasons. In commenting on this experience, he reveals his view of destiny and saving and accumulation.

"After my business failed, I gave up trying to plan my life and to get ahead. I lost the little confidence I had in myself and lived just from day to day, like an animal. I really was ashamed to make plans because I didn't have the will power to carry them out. I couldn't stick to things or follow them up. I understood others better than myself and even dared to offer suggestions to my friends about how to improve their lives. I helped them but I couldn't analyze my own problems. Concerning myself, I felt null and void.

"To me, one's destiny is controlled by a mysterious hand that moves all things. Only for the select, do things turn out as planned; to those of us who are born to be *tamale* eaters, heaven sends only *tamales*. We plan and some little thing

164

happens to wash it all away. Once I decided to try to save, and I said to Paula, 'Old girl, put away this money so that someday we'll have a little pile.' When we had ninety pesos put away, pum! my father got sick and I had to give it all to him for doctors and medicine. It was the only time I helped him and the only time I tried to save. I said to Paula, 'There you are! Why should we save if someone gets sick and we have to spend it all!' Sometimes I even think that saving brings on illness! That's why I firmly believe that some of us are born to be poor and remain that way no matter how hard we struggle and pull this way and that. God gives us just enough to go on vegetating."[10]

Manuel's father, Jesús Sánchez, grew up in a little village in the state of Vera Cruz, and worked from age eight to about fifteen as a field hand on sugar plantations. At about sixteen, he went to Mexico City where he scraped out a meager existence working as a food buyer for a restaurant. After thirty years in this work, he now earns the minimum daily wage of fourteen pesos a day or $1.12. Jesús is a man of strong opinions and he desires authoritarian solutions for the ills of Mexico.

"There are lots of cases of abandonment of children in Mexico. It happens all the time. The government should take a hand in the matter and put a stop to it. I wish we had laws in Mexico like you have in the United States. We wouldn't have so many bums. . . . All this freedom is bad for people. They should close up eighty per cent of the saloons, build more schools, close up eighty per cent of these places that breed vice. There should be more control over youngsters, over youth, rich and poor alike. . . . No bribes, a week in jail, and when it happens the second time, then

it'll take a year and you'd see how much more orderly everything would be and how the Mexican people would behave
more decently if we had stricter laws, because the laws we
have here are very loose. The Mexican people are going
under, because there's no leadership and no faith, and there's
so much lousy corruption, as you can see. . . .

"You have to live among our families to see what we
suffer from and how it can be cured. They haven't made
a thorough study of the problem. Those gentlemen who
rule over us have expensive cars and many millions in the
bank, but they don't see what's beneath where the people
live. Why, they won't even drive over to look from their
cars. They stay down there in the center of town where all
the fashionable stores are, but as for the sections where the
poor live . . . they just don't know what a miserable life
we lead. They disregard this great and deep problem which
exists in Mexico today. They disregard the fact that right
here in the capital there are lots of people who eat only one
or two meals a day.

"There is not enough money, not enough work and everything is so expensive; prices went up again today. The cost
of living has gone up a great deal within a few days.[11]

"In the thirty years I've been in Mexico City, the life of
the poor people has changed very little, very little. Some of
them call it a big change when, for example, they used to
make one or one and a half pesos during the Calles period,
which was very little, right? But then sugar and beans cost
fifteen centavos. Now take beans; you make eleven pesos and
beans cost from three to four pesos. That's a fact! So where
is the improvement?[12]

"The political gang won't let good men run. They've got
these gangs here, like everywhere. . . .

166

"And the trade-union leaders don't help either, everything right into their pockets. Take my union, one of those fellows owns one or two houses, and sixteen taxi cabs. There's nothing to hope for there. No, sir! I pay five pesos a month dues in my union. But there are lots of us, thousands. When somebody dies, we give another five pesos apiece for the family of the dead man, in addition to the five pesos every month. What do we get in return? Nothing! We haven't had a convention for years. All we get are dues slips. They deduct on payday. So if you owe for two slips, it's ten pesos. If somebody has kicked the bucket, another five pesos. So I tell the fellow, 'Does this go to the dead man or to a live person?' He says, 'A live person, of course, are you kidding?' Then I tell him, 'Listen, I don't know what you're doing with my money that you keep deducting; we're making very little and everything is so dear nowadays, so the money doesn't go far. It looks like people are dying too often here.' And that's the way it goes.[13]

"Things must be different in the United States. Well, maybe it's better that we just have one gang running the country here, because it's got a pistol in each hand. Don't you know this story about two fellows who were playing cards and one had two aces and the other fellow asks him, 'What do you have?' 'Two aces. And you?' 'Two pistols.' So he says, 'O.K., you win.' And that's the way the PRI is here; it's got the pistols and anybody who objects, well, he gets run over by a car. . . .

"There's nothing dirtier than politics. It's pretty rotten, and there's been a lot of bloodshed too, and who knows what else. How many people die so a man can get into power? . . . Of course, the people have no education, they're ignorant, they're like a flock following wherever the shepherd leads them. He tells them, you go this way, and they go this way, you go that way, and they go that way. You should see how they act in the unions when there's a meeting. They tell them this, that, and the other. All those in favor? Everybody votes in favor. They don't even know what they voted in favor of. . . .

"They listen to the fellow who's on top, sitting behind the desk, even though he's not doing them any good, see? Then they applaud him. So how are you going to straighten things out? What can you do?

"Now besides all of that, the Mexican people have no unity, they're not united. One pulls in one direction, the other in another and so on. If people would unite, in union there's strength, they say, then things would change. I know in other countries, if they don't like a president, they toss a nice little bomb and you have a different president. Not here. That's what they should do here, but they don't. A bit of cyanide, a heart attack, yes, there's what many of our presidents and governors and police chiefs need. Well, it's not nice to say so and admit it because they are my compatriots, eh? They're Mexicans, but like I told you a little while ago, the truth will always get out."[14]

Finally, Consuelo, age twenty-seven, the eldest daughter, analyzes the various members of her family with considerable insight. She has had eight years of school and is the most literate, most ambitious, most sensitive, and, also, the most disruptive person in the Sánchez family.

"When I thought of my sister and my brothers, I became bitter, for not one of them would or could help me. Of the three, Manuel had the hardest heart. He was never there when he was needed and even if he were, nothing concerned him. He reminded me of a person walking backwards in darkness, without setting foot upon solid ground. He walked and walked and got nowhere. He just moved his legs to give people the impression he was doing something. His gaze was fixed upon little stars shining in the firmament. He tried to catch them and when he managed to get one, he would sit down there in the infinite emptiness and play with it until the dazzling light lost its power. Then he would leave the dead star floating in the air and go irresistibly after another.

"He never looked to either side or downward, because if he did, he would see the dark abyss beneath him. He was in dread of falling; if he ever reached the ground, he would feel how rugged and hard is the road where people walk. So he looked upward to the heavens, not to implore, but to make loud excuses when he fell. 'I didn't see . . . I didn't know.'

"Maybe he was afraid of being judged or smashed down, or of finding that he had no salvation. Maybe that was why he had two or three personalities and many faces. He tried to show that he had an invincible worldly quality, but it was a lie. He was only superficial and cynical. He had a spark of generosity and appreciation in him, perhaps because he had known his mother's and Paula's love, but why wasn't he more human? He knew the damage he did, but under no circumstances would he say, 'Yes, I did it.'

"Why did he show such fury when he was in a fight and yet turn his back when he had to face problems that came up? He claimed he loved Paula very much. Then why didn't he marry her? When a Latin really wants to capture some illusion, whether out of vanity or caprice, the first thing he will do is get married. He managed to be a winner in card playing, why then, when his father gave him the opportunity of setting up a shoe shop, didn't he come out on top? If he studied up on gambling, why didn't he take the same trouble to find out the value of a nail, for example? Why?

"And why did he always have to be shirking responsibilities? He closed his eyes to everything. Any idea of unity or aid from him was impossible. When I was in trouble he said to me, 'The day you need help, don't count on me. If I happen to see you someday in a cabaret, just assume that I'm not your brother, that you don't even know me.' In his egotism, he was unable to feel anything deeply, even being a father. His life was completely free and he defended his liberty for everything. With Manuel, liberty had become an abominable vice.[15]

"Roberto was the best of the three. He would say, 'I'm sorry for you, sister. I'm a man and can go any place, but what can you do?' He was generous, sympathetic, and truly sincere, but he had no money and no real home either. And what a child! He was violent and still had temper tantrums. He imagined he was a Samson who could demolish whole battalions. Compared with Manuel, he was pure emotion, although the emotional circle in which he whirled about was infantile.

"Even though Roberto was a man, he walked along the highway of life like a child of eight or nine, in knee-pants, short-sleeved shirt and heavy boots. He was a frightened child whose intelligence had been side-tracked by the broken road. His way was full of accidents and he had fallen countless times, leaving him deeply scarred. He walked with his right hand stretched out, trying to reach something . . . the shadowy form of a woman . . . which floated before

170

him. He wept and cried out, calling to that thing to stop. Occasionally it disappeared and that was when Roberto threw himself to the ground in a tantrum.

"He kicked the stones, beat them, and threw them away because they seemed to be mocking him. He would get angry and say, 'Who are these to make fun of me! I'll show them who I am!' He didn't realize that he would get hurt colliding against the rocks. When his tantrum passed, he regretted having smashed himself so stubbornly. Now he would think, 'They were only looking at me.'

"In contrast to Manuel, Roberto had a fixed goal . . . to find the security he needed. When he has finally found it, the sobbing will end and he will smile as he looks back over the whole course he covered. Then, with 'it,' he will take a new road. Roberto was a good boy, so long as he had someone to pay attention to his problems, to listen to his complaints, join in his pleasures, and give him advice about how to dress. In spite of everything, he had a docility, a sensitivity of feeling that was foreign to Manuel.

"The hardest, bitterest, saddest time of Roberto's life was when he was in jail. I know of many people who come out brutalized and hardened and filled with hatred. Not my brother. He always kept alive that tiny flame of hope and he never fell into vice. He still realized he had a family and preserved a feeling of love toward others. He was capable of taking off his own clothes to cover someone who had none, saying, 'No, poor thing, cover him up.' But Manuel! That one would probably think, 'It's none of my business; that's what he gets for being a dumb jerk.'

"Roberto looked at things with passion and tried to find his ideal. To him, no one in the world should sin. He was shocked by the things he saw, not like Manuel, who in that respect was more worldly. To Roberto, many things were sanctified and holy. No one better lay a hand on his saints, because that turned him into a devil.[16]

"The thing that made me saddest about my brothers and sister was that they did not wish to get out of the situation in which they lived. They were satisfied to have poor clothes and to spend their time fighting. To me, the low roof which covered us was insecure, for tomorrow the pillar supporting it could fall. But they didn't think of tomorrow. They all lived in the present.

"And even if they tried to change, I don't believe they could. None of them, perhaps myself included although I meant to try, seemed to have the right qualities of character. For example, if someone gave Manuel a common stone, he would hold it in his hand and look at it eagerly. In a few seconds, it would begin to shine and he would see that it was made of silver, then of gold, then of the most precious things imaginable, until the glitter died out.

"Roberto would hold the same stone and would murmur, 'Hmmm. What is this good for?' But he wouldn't know the answer.

"Marta would hold it in her hand for just a moment, and without a thought, would throw it carelessly away.

"I, Consuelo, would look at it wonderingly. 'What might this be? Is it, could it be, what I have been looking for?'

"But my father would take the stone and set it on the ground. He would look for another and put it on top of the first one, then another and another, until no matter how long it took, he had finally turned it into a house."[17]

All citations below refer to the author's *The Children of Sánchez: Autobiography of a Mexican Family*. (New York: Random House, 1961).

1. Pages xxiv-xxv.
2. Page xxv.
3. Pages xxvi-xxvii.
4. Page xxvii.
5. Pages 38-39.
6. Page 336.
7. Pages 338-39.
8. Page 339.
9. Pages 339-40.
10. Page 171.
11. Pages 493-94.
12. Page 495.
13. Page 496.
14. Pages 498-99.
15. Pages 271-72.
16. Pages 272-74.
17. Page 274.

THE ALLIANCE
FOR
PROGRESS

GEORGE I. BLANKSTEN

One would probably be well advised to define his terms before embarking on a larger discussion of the problems facing the Alliance for Progress. The term "foreign aid" has been very loosely used in this country. There are, of course, understandable reasons for confusion in use of the term. The press has not tended to distinguish between various types of foreign aid, and the Congress of the United States very frequently makes provisions for more than one type of foreign aid in the same bill. Against this background, there has been a tendency in the United States and in some of the other American republics to become confused about the nature of foreign aid.

It is necessary that one be able to distinguish among different kinds of programs that are brought together under this same umbrella. There are, for example, programs of military assistance that are called foreign aid. The United States also has programs of economic and technical assistance, both of which fall into this category. While these programs are often similarly designated, they are quite different from one another in nature and often in objectives. It is important, therefore, to make certain distinctions. The purpose of military aid is quite different from that of technical assistance. Military aid has a short-run political objective; the success or failure of a military-aid program is much easier to evaluate than in some other programs. Economic aid as a part of the foreign-aid program has been addressed on different occasions to different types of objectives. The United States has sometimes sponsored programs of economic aid as emergency assistance, stop-gap programs of one type or another.

Technical assistance, on the other hand, while it is also foreign aid, has been quite different in terms of its orientations. Technical-assistance programs have long-run, developmental objectives that look to gradual rises in the standards of living of the various participating countries. A technical-assistance program in agriculture, for example, might have as its objective the development of more effective farming techniques leading to the production of more food per acre of land. Or a program of technical assistance in industrial production might teach aspiring entrepreneurs in a developing country some useful techniques in the organization of new industries.

Confusion among these different types of foreign aid led to interesting situations in the administration of foreign aid in the days before the establishment of the Alliance for Progress. For example, there have been times when each of the three types of United States programs—military as-

sistance, economic aid, technical assistance—was administered separately by a different agency, each pursuing its own
path and its own set of objectives. Thus, emergency economic aid designed to help a country stricken by a crop failure or food shortage has on occasion been made available
to a country which was, at the same time, participating in a
technical-assistance program in agricultural development,
with each of these types of aid functioning independently of
the other.

The government has also had periods when all three types
of programs were joined together in one administrative
agency, which then attempted to co-ordinate the three in one
fashion or another.

Probably the outstanding illustration of the latter type of
administration came during the period of the Foreign Operations Administration (FOA), an agency of the United States
government that operated in the two-year period between
1953 and 1955 under the leadership of Harold Stassen.
During Stassen's administration, the FOA administered all
three types of foreign aid in terms of the definitions and the
objectives of the military-assistance program. Thus, economic aid and technical assistance during that period served
the short-run political objectives of military aid. In this
period many people devoted to the problems of economic
development in Latin America and to problems of standards
of living and of economic change objected violently to sub-
jecting technical-assistance programs to military-aid objectives. Partly for that reason, the FOA was abolished in 1955
to make way for a new pattern of organization under the
International Co-operation Administration (ICA). A State
Department agency, the ICA administered technical assistance

on the part of the United States in an administrative context, separating it from both military aid and economic aid.

Today, in the Alliance for Progress, there is a new kind of combination of certain forms of the long-standing foreign-aid programs of the United States. The Alliance has joined economic aid with technical assistance. These had been united once before in the days of the FOA, but at that time technical assistance, that is developmental assistance, was made to serve the objective of the other aid programs. Under the Alliance for Progress, that portion of economic aid which is made a part of the Alliance is made to serve the ends of technical assistance. There is now economic aid directed toward technological innovation, economic growth, and improvement in the standard of living in Latin America. In a sense, technical assistance plays the part of the "dog" rather than the "tail." In terms of governmental policies, many of the components of the Alliance for Progress are fairly old. What is new in the Alliance is, in the first place, the recombination of types of foreign aid of such a nature that the aid programs within the Alliance are at the service of developmental growth objectives rather than short-run political objectives. In the second place, there has been an attempt through the Alliance for Progress to accomplish these aims on a wider multilateral basis than had existed in the past. The United States has attempted, through OAS meetings at Punta del Este and elsewhere, to obtain multilateral participation in the Alliance on the part of all the American republics.

As it is conceived, the Alliance for Progress is a ten-year program of economic development in the Americas within this multilateral framework. It should be pointed out that

178

since economic aid is now related to economic development and technological change, the governments which participate in programs of the Alliance for Progress are required to establish a favorable climate for certain internal social and economic reforms. This will insure that economic assistance will relate more effectively to growth and development in the countries involved. Economic aid in the form of a grant or loan of a sum of money would now be used, for example, for the purchase of technical or industrial equipment needed to carry out a growth project developed through technical assistance.

Under the arrangements for the Alliance, there is a procedure by which certain developmental plans are recommended to the participating governments by the Inter-American Economic and Social Council and by other agencies. When participating governments become interested enough in some of the proposals for developmental plans to pursue them further, requests are made by the governments involved for studies by teams of experts, who are provided by such agencies as the International Monetary Fund. These teams make studies of the economies of the countries and bring reports before the Committee of Nine which is elected by the members of the Alliance for Progress. This committee has been dubbed, fortunately or unfortunately, "the Nine Wise Men." This group first reviews the developmental plans brought in by study teams. Then the government involved is invited to review the recommendations approved by the "Nine Wise Men." If the government still wishes to pursue the plan, then foreign aid is made available for development.

The Alliance has encountered many problems in its initial phases, but the program also has its strengths. Since most of its problems will be examined in this essay, some passing attention should be paid to the strong points of the *Alianza.*

The basic idea is a sound one. While there have been problems and mistakes in administration and occasionally in the selection of personnel, and in spite of the feeling that the United States might be doing the right thing in the wrong way, the central notion of the program is correct. If economic development is seen as technological change designed to derive a greater output or a higher standard of living from an economy, what the Alliance for Progress does essentially is to relate more of the resources of economic aid to this developmental objective. If the Alliance is successful in stimulating and contributing to economic development in the participating countries, this will be a major step in improving the economic relations of the United States with the other American republics.

Some theoretical questions remain unanswered, and a few are fundamental. For example, assuming that the Alliance for Progress should contribute to economic development in some of the participating countries, what then would be the relationship between economic growth, on the one hand, and political change, on the other? This is a question which has elicited few hard, sound answers. There are, of course, various kinds of political change, one being violent revolution. Would economic development, if it were really to take hold in one of the countries involved, lead to some kind of political revolution? There are many who are committed to this view.

There are others, including many economists, who take the view that the relationship is exactly the opposite—that there are certain political prerequisites for economic development and that political revolution is a proper stimulus for a later rapid economic development. Those who take this view sometimes point to the Mexican revolution as a political stimulus to economic development.[1] There are also those, like the political scientist K. H. Silvert, who think of economic development as an alternative to political revolution in many of the underdeveloped countries of Latin America.[2] Any of these theories is likely to be true depending on the circumstances involved. Intellectual sophistication in the theoretical aspects of relating certain types of political changes, such as revolution, to economic development has not yet reached the predictive stage. The circumstances in which there would be one kind of relationship between economic development and political revolution as opposed to the circumstances in which there might be other relationships cannot as yet be spelled out with certainty. Still, in spite of these theoretical problems, the basic principles of the Alliance are sound.

The Alliance for Progress is also faced with frustrating obstacles in its operation. There has been only a small tendency for the specific programs undertaken under the name of the Alliance to be related to one another. A housing project has been undertaken in a given country without reference to an educational program in the same locality. Both are needed and, indeed, each, in isolation from the other, is useful. But they would be more effective if they were interrelated to create a greater developmental result from the separate efforts.

The Alliance still is in danger of being something of an omnibus operation, where great numbers of small foreign-aid projects are begun without giving much thought to the relationship of these projects to economic development and to the Alliance as a whole. The Alliance would be more effective if there were some integration of the various, presently unco-ordinated programs. In most cases co-ordination could be accomplished without much difficulty and without any great damage to vested interests that have become involved in the Alliance. Such co-ordination must be effected if the Alliance is to be more effective.

A second type of problem which the Alliance faces is the intransigence of different elite groups in Latin America. There are governments which are reluctant to make the internal social and economic reforms proposed by study teams and by the "Nine Wise Men." Critics may say this was to have been expected and point out that governing groups always resist change. In Latin America, however, two types of elites exist. There are the groups which resist change and which regard economic development or other forms of change as threats to their traditional controlling position. Thus, landowner's associations may resist agrarian reform, a church hierarchy may oppose steps toward a greater separation of church and state, or a group of army officers may resist attempts to free civilian government from military control in a situation of political militarism. On the other hand, some governing groups welcome change, seek to promote it, and attempt to guide, to plan for, and to stimulate it.

Some governing groups in Latin American countries are frequently under pressures to produce change. For example, a revolutionary government is usually required to show that life since the revolution is different from what it had been before. To think of the governing groups as being opposed to change, especially in the more rapidly changing countries

182

where the new elite desires a new order and finds itself opposing the older elite that is still wedded to the status quo, is woefully inaccurate and unrealistic.

In some Latin American countries, the *Alianza para Progreso* has become subject of jest: "Alianzi si; progreso no." Statements such as these have resulted from objection to reform. Some plans for development, for example, have suggested tax reform or the introduction of income tax into areas where it has been unknown. Some programs have proposed land reforms which are often resisted by the countries involved. In fact, some Latin American governments have sought to obtain economic aid without making reforms. Requests have been presented which have said, in effect, "We do not have time to make the reforms, but we need the money in a hurry." So far the administration of the Alliance has resisted such pressures, but they are serious, nonetheless. At the end of the first year and a half of the Alliance for Progress, only five of the nineteen Latin American governments eligible to participate in this program agreed to make the internal social and economic reforms recommended by study teams and supported by the Committee of Nine.

Another problem is the failure of one of the administrative agencies given a major role in the operation of the Alliance for Progress to function effectively. This is the Inter-American Economic and Social Council (IA-ECOSOC), established as one of the major organs of the Organization of American States (OAS). Emerging as a leading analyst on this problem of the IA-ECOSOC is Professor John N. Plank of the Fletcher School of Law and Diplomacy, who participated some years ago in a study of the OAS prepared for the subcommittee on American republic affairs of the Senate Foreign Relations

Committee. Plank has recently prepared an intensive study of IA-ECOSOC, pointing in great detail to some of its problems. This agency, for example, has such a great turnover in the delegates at its meetings that the overwhelming majority of the delegates present at a given annual meeting had not attended any previous meeting. Partly for this reason, IA-ECOSOC has developed very little sense of continuity. At the typical IA-ECOSOC meeting, most of the delegates are there for the first time; they have little sense of what has been done in the past or even of the history of economic development in the Americas. When a proposal is put before them, they seldom know whether it is a new idea, or whether it was proposed last year as well.[3] The unsatisfactory functioning of IA-ECOSOC stands today as another of the major problems in the operation of the Alliance for Progress.

It is not easy at this stage to evaluate the Alliance in such flat terms as "Is it a success?" or "Is it a failure?" One of the problems is failure to place its operation in perspective. It should be remembered that this is a ten-year program. The gentleman who is the United States co-ordinator for the Alliance, Ambassador Teodoro Moscoso, has tended to worry publicly about the Alliance. Articles have appeared in various periodicals with such titles as, "Will the Alliance for Progress Ever Get Off the Ground?" or "Does the *Alianza* Have a Chance?" One of the things that is interesting about these articles is that some of them are written or inspired by Moscoso himself. This has had a healthy effect in achieving a public realization that the Alliance faces difficult problems; but on the other hand, it is not fair at this stage to write the *Alianza* off as a failure. Within a year and a half only five of the nineteen eligible countries have approved plans for reforms which, in turn, will prepare these states for the next stage in the *Alianza* program. But against the ten-year perspective, it may well be that having come this far within the first fraction of the program is not a bad showing.

1. Robert E. Scott, *Mexican Government in Transition* (Urbana, Ill., 1959), *passim;* and George I. Blanksten, "Modernization and Revolution in Latin America" (unpublished manuscript, 1962).

2. K. H. Silvert, *The Conflict Society* (New Orleans, 1962), *passim.*

3. See Northwestern University, *The Organization of American States* (Washington, D. C., 1959), *passim;* and John N. Plank, "The Inter-American Economic and Social Council" (unpublished manuscript, 1962).

NOTES ON
THE
CONTRIBUTORS

GEORGE I. BLANKSTEN is professor of political science at Northwestern University. He is the author of *Ecuador: Constitutions and Caudillos* (1951); *Peron's Argentina* (1953); and *The United States' Role in Latin America* (1961). He has taught at the Universidad Nacional Autonoma de Mexico as well as at several American universities; and he has served as a political analyst with the United States Office of Inter-American Affairs.

DAVID D. BURKS is professor of history at the University of Michigan, in Dearborn. He has also taught at Otterbein College and Oakland University; and in the year 1962-63, he held a research grant at the Council on Foreign Relations in New York City, where he was engaged in the study of Fidel Castro and his government in Cuba.

THOMAS F. CARROLL is the chief of the Agricultural Development Group in the Inter-American Development Bank in Washington, D. C. He served in the past with the Food and Agricultural Organization of the United Nations, both at its headquarters in Rome and on field assignments in Latin America, and has taught at the University of California at Berkeley and in the Graduate School of Economics of the University of Chile in Santiago.

SYDNEY NETTLETON FISHER is co-ordinator of the Graduate Institute for World Affairs and professor of history at the Ohio State University. He served as editor of the *Middle East Journal* in 1953, is the author of several books, and has edited several volumes of essays, including *Social Forces in the Middle East* (Ithaca, N. Y.: Cornell University Press, 1955) and *The Military in the Middle East: Problems in Society and Government* (Columbus, O.: Ohio State University Press, 1963).

JOHN P. HARRISON is director of the Institute of Latin American Studies and professor of history at the University of Texas. He has gained wide experience in Latin American affairs from many years with the Rockefeller Foundation.

JOHN J. KENNEDY is professor of foreign affairs at the University of Virginia. He has also taught at the University of Puerto Rico and the University of Notre Dame, and for a number of years was a regional specialist in the Department of State. He is the author of *Catholicism, Nationalism and Democracy in Argentina* (Notre Dame, Ind.: University of Notre Dame Press, 1958).

188

OSCAR LEWIS is professor of anthropology at the University of Illinois. He is the author of *The Children of Sánchez: Autobiography of a Mexican Family* (New York: Random House, 1961) and *Five Families* (New York: Basic Books, 1959).

EDWIN LIEUWEN is professor of history at the University of New Mexico. He has also taught at the University of California, both at Los Angeles and Berkeley, and the University of Utrecht; was an exchange scholar in Venezuela; and served as an officer of the Department of State. He is the author of *Arms and Politics in Latin America* (New York: Frederick A. Praeger, 1960), which appeared the same year in Argentina in Spanish translation.

ARNOLD E. SCHAEFER is executive director of the Interdepartmental Committee on Nutrition for National Defense of the National Institutes of Health. He has recently been engaged in research in nutrition at the University of Wisconsin and the Alabama Polytechnic Institute, and for four years was head of the department for nutrition research at the Squibb Institute for medical research. He has been active in conducting surveys on nutrition in many foreign countries, including Peru, Ecuador, Chile, Colombia, Uruguay, and Bolivia.

JOHN J. TEPASKE is assistant professor of history at the Ohio State University. He is co-editor of *The Character of Philip II: The Problem of Moral Judgments in History*; has done research in various archives in Spain, England, Peru,

Bolivia, and Chile concerning various aspects of colonial Hispanic America; and has carried on post-doctoral study at the University of California, Berkeley.

194